MW01002212

Sexual Bewitchery

Sexual Bewitchery

AND OTHER ANCIENT FEMININE WILES

BARRIE DOLNICK, JULIA CONDON
AND DONNA LIMOGES

ILLUSTRATED BY JULIA CONDON

AVON BOOKS  NEW YORK

Avon Books
A division of
The Hearst Corporation
1350 Avenue of the Americas
New York, New York 10019

Interior design by Kellan Peck
Illustrations by Julia Condon
Visit our website at **http://www.AvonBooks.com**
ISBN: 0-380-97573-4

Library of Congress Cataloging in Publication Data:

Dolnick, Barrie.
Sexual bewitchery : and other ancient feminine wiles / Barrie Dolnick, Julia Condon, and Donna Limoges.—1st ed.
p. cm.
Includes bibliographical references.
1. Sex—Miscellanea. 2. Magic. I. Condon, Julia. II. Limoges, Donna. III. Title.
BF1623.S4D65 1998 97-33167
306.7—dc21 CIP

First Avon Books Printing: February 1998

Printed in the U.S.A.

FIRST EDITION

QPM 10 9 8 7 6 5 4 3 2 1

This book is dedicated
to the resurrection of
ancient feminine knowledge.

ACKNOWLEDGMENTS

We thank GlenMaera for invaluable help and wish her well in the next phase of her journey.

Thanks to the Curleys and the magic of Onteora for a sacred and beautiful space in which to write.

Gratitude to Christine Zika for her dedication, and to Emma Sweeney for believing in us and the magic.

And to the people we love for their patience and support and faith.

CONTENTS

PREFACE

Love and desire cannot be measured by science, psychology, or even your best friend. Love is just plain mysterious.

There are no rules where love is concerned. Why bother manipulating and faking it when you can naturally have him eating out of your hand (or better yet, feeding you delicately with his)?

Sexual Bewitchery and other Ancient Feminine Wiles teaches you to use what you've got, guides you to your ancient feminine knowledge, and reinforces both the satisfaction of being a woman and pride in your powers.

Your power to beguile is within you already. It's not so obvious, though; women's sensual power is subtle; it is the power of enticement and allure.

Why get yourself into a tizzy by asking hundreds of your friends for advice about how to get that guy, look good, be great in bed, revive a boring relationship, or get out of one? The answers are not the same for everyone—there is no formula. You'll feel more confident about what you want and how to get it when you use your feminine powers. Women's preferences are highly individual.

Sexual Bewitchery and other Ancient Feminine Wiles revives your inborn knowledge of the ancient feminine arts and resurrects your mysterious magical powers of attraction, seduction and wisdom.

Whether you are married or single, involved or alone, we encourage you to use your feminine wiles and make them a part of everyday life.

The power of the feminine is within your grasp.

INTRODUCTION

Shadows cast
and room aglow
Woman is power;
that men know.
Soft in touch
but hot with fire
Woman roil ecstasy
higher and higher.

Seductress, Vixen, Enchantress, Sorceress, Charmer, Siren.

Which one are you?

No easy answer? No wonder!

We've forgotten, lost, or otherwise abandoned a truly feminine power: *seduction!*

Enough whining and moaning about how men do us wrong. We've got the power to do and have what we want in a relationship. Unfortunately, most of us have forgotten how to use that power. We don't even realize that our ancient feminine heritage is still alive and well inside that GAP-clad unisex world of ours.

We will set you back on track by helping you realize your feminine power and how to use it. This process requires only a few initial changes:

- Leave your corporate strategy in the office.
- Stop trying to be like a man (for Goddess's sake, you're not).
- Trade in your cell phone for some quiet time.
- Add a lunar calendar to your Filofax.
- Don't use CNN for all your info; try tuning in to your intuition.
- Escape the concrete jungle and suburban sprawl with a walk in the park.

You need to remember that your feminine power is with you everywhere you go. The source of the feminine is all around you—in nature, the moon, the earth. You can amplify this power with scents, colors, and flowers to make it more real to you and others. The more you notice and bring nature into your life, the more natural using your feminine powers will be. Don't worry, you won't be trailing scarves and scent wherever you go. Your feminine allure will parallel your own personal style. Katharine Hepburn was sexy and she didn't get too frilly.

Lest you're concerned that you need to join a coven or buy a caldron to be bewitching, rest assured you don't have to be within the witch tradition to do this. Every woman is born with mystery: the magic of creation, allure, and magnetism. It's such an innate force you don't even notice it, which simply means that you're not using it to its fullest potential. Bewitchery is the power to enchant, and all women have that within them. You just need to focus it.

The feminine archetype has been around since prehistory:

it is that of the vessel, the mother, the fertile holder of potential. You can embrace any and all parts of this nature. Just don't ignore it, or you leave behind your mystical powers. Women really are the true creators, who give birth to reality, and men are the manifestors, who build reality. It is more powerful to work with what comes naturally, than to try to do both. Women are just better at intuition and creativity, the yin, a more receptive energy; while men are better at the scientific and practical, the yang, an action-oriented energy.

Even if you have to fight for recognition or reward in your job, don't stop being a woman. You are much more effective using your feminine energy, than trying to emulate a man. (If nothing else, men react better to women as women than to women acting as men.)

Also, forget what the fashion magazines tell you; there is not just one look for a woman—it doesn't exist. You don't have to be young to be beautiful, or thin, for that matter. The older you get the more intriguing you become, which is an allure many men enjoy. Really. Just think about it, it's the difference between a novel and a short story—a novel needs more time to develop the plot and interest.

Sexual Bewitchery tells you how to use your emotional, passionate, intellectual, physical, and psychic energy to heighten sensual and sexual pleasure in your life, to attract, to tease, to play with men.

This book isn't just about sex; it is about the magic of allure and enticement.

To illustrate our point, we'll turn to our favorite screen stars. Consider the old movie stars whose allure was strong without flaunting their bodies; sex appeal without a sledgehammer versus their current counterparts.

Today	Yesterday	Persona
Madonna	Marilyn Monroe	Sexy sirens
Goldie Hawn	Carole Lombard	Dizzy dames
Sharon Stone	Marlene Dietrich	Tough cookies
Julia Roberts	Rita Hayworth	Femme fatales
Demi Moore	Sophia Loren	Lusty dishes

First of all, if you haven't heard of or seen the stars of yesteryear, go to the video store, now. You'll learn a lot just by watching them.

The difference between today's female stars and those of the past is obvious: the art of seduction, repartee, and flirtation was far more important in the past. They didn't have to buy new breasts or go without underwear to get a guy, and neither do you.

Allure is a fabulous sexual magnet, and half the fun of physical pleasure is the anticipation of arriving at your goal. You can create mystery, passion, secrecy, immediacy, and risk (safely) by knowing what to use and how to use it.

What if I'm not in a relationship?

You don't have to have a partner. (We like to call him a consort.) We'll give you the tools and techniques to attract any number of eligible suitors.

Do I have to be psychic?

No, you just have to be a woman with a pulse. We don't think they've identified the "bewitching" gene, but it's there, somewhere. We've all got it and we'll help you find yours. (And no, it is not as elusive as a G spot.)

Will this change the nature of how I have sex?

We believe you'll use this book forever. Enough said?

Do I have to learn to twitch my nose?

Nah. It's too obvious. We'll give you more subtle magic.

Do I have to become a fragile, fainting flower?

Absolutely not. Being feminine does not mean kowtowing to anyone or tying yourself to the railroad tracks. Using your feminine bewitchery means you draw what you want to you, how you do that is up to you. This power gives you the ability to be vulnerable and soft without giving anything away.

Sexual Bewitchery reacquaints you with your innate feminine conjuring talents so you can enjoy sensual and sexual pleasures. You'll use scents, colors, fabrics, even foods, to fuel psychic means of attraction.

With our exercises you'll be able to heighten your pleasure and his, not to mention learn how to refresh your love life with new and daring scenarios. You'll also learn to solve any problems you might come across in your amorous pursuits. You'll be a full-fledged psychic seductress in no time.

Sexual Bewitchery

As *with sweet leaves*
As *with subtle clearness*
Oh, I *have picked up magic*
In *her nearness.*

—EZRA POUND, A VIRGINAL

ONE

Bewitching Tools of the Trade

Sex is all too often reduced to getting it on and getting it off. We haven't yet met a woman who likes it that way. (And men don't either once they know better.) Your bewitching arts can transform the same old "bump and grind" into something truly original.

Seduce, tantalize, tease, linger. Take the time to enjoy yourself. With your new sensual powers, your consort will beg for more and you'll be happy to oblige him.

First things first: forget the black hat, broomstick, or any other cliché witch accessory. That's what men think when they think

of witches. Silly them. The real tools of sexual bewitchery are those that make you sensual, beautiful, enticing, and delightful.

Is it going to be hard? Good Goddess no. You're already using your feminine powers; you just don't realize it. Every time you put on perfume, sexy underwear, or mood music, you're shifting into sensual magic. Every time you plot and plan (and we know you do) you are trying to make something happen.

You'll have more success and time to spend on enjoying him when you use your natural, magical powers. You're not making a major change in your routine, just shifting your intention.

Mirror, Mirror on the Wall

Are you the fairest one of all? To him you can be because lasting attraction has little to do with physical perfection. But you have to be able to look in the mirror with your Inner Sight. That means seeing beyond the obvious reflection and looking with your heart, not your eyes. Your Inner Sight is your intuition, what you sense, not what you see.

Are you aware of energy you're giving off? Do you know when you're sexy or when you're not at your best? Do you know how to shift this? Just putting on lipstick doesn't do it.

We all project an image of the kind of woman we are or think we are, whether we are paying attention to it or not. These signals are received and acted on by others (especially men).

Try an immediate experiment. Walk down a hallway or down the street and think, "I'm sexy and attractive." Walk in a relaxed manner, don't be afraid to meet the glances you are sure to attract and certainly don't be afraid there won't be any. Expect them; this is part of your power to enchant. You always have the choice of tuning it up or down according to your desires plus the right to accept or reject.

Remember this is fun and exhilarating. If you're not in the mood, stop and try again another day. With a few tips and some practice, you'll just be doing what comes naturally. Walking with your sexiness is a fabulously bewitching morale booster available at any time.

BAT: Bewitching Aptitude Test

Let's see how much of an enchantress you are already. Choose one answer for each question.

Scenario: You're seeing your man and are in the mood to be passionate.

1. Choose one of the following scents.
   - *a.* Lily of the Valley
   - *b.* Jasmine
   - *c.* Peach
   - *d.* Lavender
2. What color will you choose to wear? (No, you can't choose black, yet.)
   - *a.* Pastels (pink, powder blue, pale yellow)
   - *b.* Earth tones (russet, gold, sand)
   - *c.* Jewel tones (ruby red, sapphire blue, emerald green)
   - *d.* Neutrals (gray, taupe, beige)
3. What outfit will you choose?
   - *a.* Pantsuit
   - *b.* Jeans, silk tee-shirt (jacket optional)

c. Miniskirt
d. Ankle-length dress (slit optional)

Scenario: You are making dinner for your consort (whether he is new or has been around for a while), and you're in the mood for seduction.

4. In the hour before he comes, what are you doing? (Now be honest!)
   a. Trying on several outfits
   b. Cleaning up your place
   c. Calling your friends for advice
   d. Setting the table
5. Your atmosphere includes:
   a. Candles
   b. Candles, soft music
   c. Candles, soft music, sexy outfit
   d. Candles, soft music, sexy outfit, champagne and strawberries on floor, with cushions piled up
6. For little nibbles before or after dinner (Who says you ever get to dinner . . . ?):
   a. Chips and dip
   b. Mixed nuts
   c. Cheese and fruit
   d. Oysters on the half shell
7. Flowers in the room are
   a. Red roses
   b. White lilies
   c. Carnations
   d. Gardenias
8. How do you get him into bed?
   a. Take his hand and lead him there in silence

b. Who needs a bed?
c. Recline on the sofa with peak of breast or leg
d. Disappear and let him find you in bed

Scoring

Add up your points as follows.

1.	a. 1	b. 3	c. 0	d. 2	5.	a. 2	b. 3	c. 1	d. 0
2.	a. 2	b. 3	c. 3	d. 1	6.	a. 0	b. 3	c. 2	d. 1
3.	a. 0	b. 2	c. 1	d. 3	7.	a. 2	b. 0	c. 1	d. 3
4.	a. 2	b. 1	c. 0	d. 3	8.	a. 3	b. 3	c. 3	d. 3

Here's How You Rate

0–10 You really need us.
11–20 You're showing promise—this won't be hard at all.
21+ We can help you hone your already bewitching behavior.

Understanding Your BAT

1. Choosing a Fragrance

A scent is a way of speaking without words, so say the right thing. Not that we have anything against the fragrance industry, but when it comes to perfume we've learned the importance of simplicity. Most fragrances on the market today blend too many messages, and no good practitioner of the feminine arts would wear those that did not whisper of love and desire. Dab on a bit of our suggested scents on secret spots to help guide him along.

With a little fragrance, you'll feel your energy and mood change. Suddenly you're mysterious or passionate, innocent or tarty. Use it as your starting point before you get dressed. Take heed if you start to feel like an old lady, that one's not for you.

Here are some particulars from the quiz.

- **Peach** won't arouse him, and passion will be a fruitless venture—literally. Fruit-related fragrances send out no message at all except for the flowers of orange and lemon, which make love blossom.
- **Lily of the valley** is fine for inspiration, but it won't help your love life. (It improves mental ability.)
- **Lavender** might lull your consort into a good mood but it won't help his passions match (or exceed) yours.
- **Jasmine** hits all the right notes and heightens your allure. This surely will raise more than his interest!

Use fragrance to tantalize, entice, and draw him closer. The mystical woman orchestrates her scents to attract, heighten passion, and raise her own feelings of sensuality. Leaving perfumed love notes—on the pillow, in his clothes, will evoke the memory of your shared passion long after the evening is done.

2. Choosing a Color

The color you wear doesn't just set off your beautiful eyes or match your socks. Colors create atmospheres of excitement, power, fragility, and touchability. They send subliminal messages. Colors also resonate with your personal energy to enhance or cool down qualities you already have. Glinda the Good Witch from the Wizard of Oz wore icy blue for clarity and purity; those were her work clothes. Scarlett O'Hara did wonders in red; there was no doubt about her fiery nature.

It is not difficult to master the sorcery of color, here are the basics.

When you wear a color such as taupe or beige, you are entering the neutral zone. These hues neither attract nor discourage. You can choose to send your message instead with scent, fabric, or demeanor, but used on their own, they won't give him palpitations.

Pastels are reminiscent of babies—innocent and fragile. This may be a good look if you can pull it off *but,* keep in mind you could also look like a sorbet: sweet and icy or like Glinda, good but untouchable. We don't suggest this for beginners.

Jewel tones come and go in fashion but are always perfect for sensual witchery. These colors are powerful but approachable. Ruby red, emerald green, sapphire blue, to name a few, are all attractive and magnetic. It takes a confident man to approach a woman in royal colors.

Earth tones such as terra cotta, red-browns, and golden yellows don't mean you are an earth mother. They are the feminine colors of sex. Their warmth invites his touch. Most skilled women of magic find a way to weave these colors into their wardrobes, through underwear, scarves, and mixing them with neutrals. You can wear a drop-dead gorgeous black dress and drape a cinnamon-colored shawl over your shoulder to be both mysterious and welcoming.

Look through your closet and see which color you're using and what unconscious message you've been sending. Don't be afraid to try new colors, you can actually feel different with an accent in red or gold.

3. Clothes

When dressing for sensual pursuits, think of yourself as a gift being wrapped. Are you a care package to the hungry or an enticing birthday present? Do you come from Tiffany's, The Gap, or Frederick's of Hollywood? Bewitching clothes conjure strong magic.

Let's start with pantsuits. Think about it, for about one second. Great for an autumn walk but not for an evening of seduction. How long will it take him to tug it off of you? In most cases trousers are not advisable unless they hug your figure, are transparent, fluid, or made of luxurious fabric.

Miniskirts are short—on attention span. They're good for a quick punch but not a long, delicious follow through. Wear them to parties for flirtatious encounters, or for a casual drink when you can cross and uncross your legs. When raising the magic for a night of lovemaking, you don't want to give all your secrets away immediately. It's not as much fun when the gift isn't wrapped.

Jeans, silk tee-shirt: These are acceptable pants when styled properly—a silk tee-shirt that clings or teases your curves will offset the "unisex" look—and he'll have no questions about who is the witchy woman.

Long dress (slit optional): Jackpot! Drape and suggest, taunt and tease. Flash a bit of leg when you sit down, demurely cover it up. Don't show it, suggest it—this works with cleavage and drop backs, too. Make him hot to explore. You'll be subtly powerful.

On a general note, the wise women of ancient times wore natural fabrics, flowing and close to the skin. Picture Grecian goddess statues with their cotton, flowing robes that draped suggestively around their curves, the Egyptian women in closer-fitting sheaths that outlined their figures or the French empire costumes, which used sheer muslin and chiffon to draw attention to the breasts. When robing for erotic pleasure, remember the particular character of each fabric. At the end of this chapter we have a list to help you.

4. Preparations

We don't want you to show up at your door looking like an old washer woman. Pampering yourself is far more important than cleaning the room. Do your magic right and all he'll notice is you.

We advise you to plan ahead. It's best to know what you're wearing at least the day before. Clean and cook as much as possible in advance so the last hour is reserved for the finishing touches. Taking a fragrant bath, arranging the flowers, listening to music, or meditating are all ways to make your energy beguiling. To feel divine is to be divine.

5. Atmosphere

The atmosphere you create is an extension of you and should summon up an ambiance that reflects and enhances your mood.

Do you want bells?
Bells and whistles?
Bells, whistles, and tambourines?
Bells, whistles, tambourines, a marching band, and an ice cream sundae with a cherry on top?

We're sure you're flying along with us by now, so as to the specifics—

Candlelight is beautiful, evocative, and mysterious—in other words, perfect. Candles are important for summoning the atmosphere for your desires, as you will learn and master in Chapter 3.

Music is powerful and can fill silences comfortably. Its rhythm and melody can get you both moving in the same direction—together. Dancing is optional.

Your outfit doesn't have to scream sex, as you know. Champagne, strawberries, and cushions give too much away. Keep him guessing and let him make some moves. The enchantress entices, she doesn't grab. Allow yourselves to explore your own sensual endings. You can always have the strawberries and champagne on ice.

6. Nibbles

Food is sensual, it provides a delectable diversion as you start the evening. You can bring attention to your lips and heighten his interest when you let your hands momentarily touch. Aphrodisiacs can easily be added to the repast, if you so desire. But first you need to know what's hot and what's not.

Chips and dips are girlfriend food. It's unattractive and disaster prone. It's difficult to maintain that "come hither" aura with sour cream on your blouse. (Presenting yourself as dessert, complete with whipped cream to be licked off is an altogether different matter.)

Oysters on the half shell are too obvious and too difficult. While they are a known aphrodisiac, they don't appeal to everyone. There are many more subtle choices (see chart at end of the chapter).

Cheese and fruit are classic: simple, feminine, and elegant. You can also nourish your spell by sharing a red apple to enhance love or grapes to conjure Bacchanalian pursuits.

Mixed nuts do it all. They are easy to handle so you eat them playfully, and they symbolize abundance and earthly pleasures. You can eat in small quantities so you can save your appetite for whatever comes next.

7. Flowers

Flowers bring the beauty of nature into your boudoir, strengthening the energy of amour you have created. They remind you of your goddess side. In general, any flower that lifts your spirits is fine. We've just applied "the language of flowers" to the answers.

As beautiful as white lilies are, they are a symbol of death and resurrection. For most of us, this does not induce lust.

Carnations are good for protection, strength, and healing. If you are unsure of his reactions, they are safe. Their lightness, fragrance, and colors can be low-key additions to your atmosphere.

Red roses are fine for a steady relationship, but if he didn't give them to you, he may think someone else did; red roses are the bloom of committed passions. So for the single witch's consort, red roses could conjure pressure.

Gardenias are love flowers and are often used for spells of the heart. Since it is a more unusual choice, it is unlikely he'll know their meaning, yet he'll feel their potency.

8. Bedtime

Yes, yes, yes, and yes. If it feels good, do it, and vary it, as you wish. Be willing to be swept along by your own magic. Have fun!

The BAT (Bewitching Arts and Techniques) in Action

Here are some examples of situations in which you may use your BAT skills. Consider mixing your messages for intrigue.

If He Is Shy

Wear a fragile outfit (pastels) with a sexy scent (musk) so he is not intimidated.

If You're the One Who Is Shy

Wear a silken outfit of jewel tones to feel protected, powerful yet approachable. Mix with an orange blossom fragrance to gently attract.

If You Want to Be Direct and Bold

Go for a body-skimming, ankle-length, silk russet-colored dress with a low cut front *or* back *or* a slit up the side. Wear ylang ylang as a scent.

Mixing Business with Pleasure

Wear a dark red silk suit (no pants) and soften the look with a body suit or a chiffon tee-shirt. Wear acacia as a scent since it favors the beginning of romance.

A Word on Black and White

The distinct absence of black and white in our suggestions is deliberate and backed by good reason. White is a spiritual color; pure and ritualistic. It's not associated with virgins for nothing. If seduction is what you're after, white is only suited for situations where innocence induces passion.

As for black, the classic garb of a witch, it is the color of mystery. Black creates a blank screen; it can shield you so that others will not know what you are up to, but it can also allow others to project whatever they like onto you. While you might be shy and choose black for protection, others may see you as snooty and aloof. You can use fragrance against a backdrop of black to give off a gentle enticement, but we don't recommend using black for beginning sexual bewitchery, since you could easily be misunderstood.

How to Wow

The following pages list popular scents, colors, hues, fabrics, and foods that actually speak the language of love, sex, and sometimes, "see ya." You can use these definitions to decipher what your outfits have been saying to people all these years, whether it's been "Hey, big boy, come on up and see me sometime" or "I am not too sexy for my shirt."

Better yet, you can use this bewitching little glossary to put together combinations that express your real intention. Consciously expressing a "come hither" message in your attire can be more effective than words.

To know what works best for you, experiment. Do this only on days when you feel good about yourself and you feel secure. (A bad mood can evoke bad choices and send bad vibes.)

Experimentation is not an exact science; don't be afraid to get it wrong once in a while. There is more than one right combination of color, scent, and style. Everyone has several options that work.

When something clicks, you'll know it by feeling excited, getting compliments, feeling compelled to buy it. You may also feel endowed with a new, confident feeling of power, mystery, or sex appeal.

Essentially, this is an opportunity to use your intuition and stop believing everything magazines tell you about how you should look. Forget the age of androgyny unless you can pull it off *and* it turns you on. Let your inner wisdom override Color Me Beautiful, dress for success, or any other fashion pundit. And no matter what anyone tells you, acid colors such as chartreuse, neon orange are not easy to wear.

Glance through the following and see what catches your eye. Start here, and let your intuition guide you.

To obtain these scents you can use scented candles, incense, any other natural fragrances (no air fresheners) to carry the message.

To Entice

- **Acacia** Good for opening to situations, but not when you're in distress. Helps during the beginning phases of a romance.
- **Cedar** Gives the impression of being assured and confident. Good for meetings and first dates. Has a calming effect on the person wearing it.
- **Lavender** General scent that opens the space for connection and love.
- **Narcissus** Opens emotions and strengthens emotional identity.
- **Orange blossom** Stimulates root center to bring out your sensuality.
- **Patchouli** Evokes a sense of mystery, but with a flirtatious edge.
- **Sandalwood** Like patchouli it creates mystery plus a feeling of ancientness.
- **Vanilla** General fragrance for welcoming and warmth.

To Seduce

- **Bay** Stimulates lust, allure, and desire.
- **Bayberry** Stimulates sexual attraction/desire.

- **Cinnamon** "Heat" generator. Raises your energy and the energy of those around you.
- **Gardenia** Brings up desire.
- **Jasmine** Heightens allure for that come-hither appeal.
- **Musk** Evokes sexual stimulation. Must not be overlapped with another heavy/powerful fragrance.
- **Rose** Heart connection when you are already with someone. It has a subtle resonance.
- **Water lily** Connects your emotions to the experience.

For Lovemaking

- **Hyacinth** Connects lust and love.
- **Honeysuckle** For making love. Brings heart, throat, and brow into focus, helping to expand the lovemaking experience beyond the physical.
- **Musk** Evokes sexual stimulation. Must not be overlapped with another heavy/powerful fragrance.
- **Ylang ylang** Connects allure, love, and desire.

For Special Powers

- **Carnation** For protection if you're feeling vulnerable. Heightens emotional power. Opens energy centers but does not draw in energy from the outside.
- **Mimosa** Opens the throat and eases communications, expression.
- **Nutmeg** Balances power and emotion.
- **Violet** Increases power during breakups.

For Friendship

- **Fruits** (Peach, apricot, apple, strawberry, etc.) Nonsexual, "safe" fragrances.
- **Peppermint** For clearing only, not a sensual or sexual fragrance.
- **Verbena** Being open, light, and friendly. Better in the summer.

COLOR CONJURING: A GUIDE

Cold Colors	Messages
Lemon yellow Blue-reds Pine green Cobalt blue Violet	Aloof, remote, cool, not demure, "ice queen"

Warm Colors	Messages
Most other yellows Most reds Most other greens Sky blue Orange	Friendly, open, inviting, "come hither"

Hues

Pastels	**Messages**
Powder pink Baby blue Lemon sherbet Mint green Lavender	Young, simple, fresh icy, girlish
Earth	**Messages**
Terra-cotta Red-browns Sand	Inviting, not flirty, fertile, illuminated, warm
Neutrals	**Messages**
Taupe Gray Beige Olive Ivory	Blank, remote, "business"
Jewel	**Messages**
Ruby Sapphire Topaz Emerald Amethyst	Clear, direct, rich, touchable, reverent

YOUR MAGIC ROBES: THE POWER OF FABRIC

Before he caresses your skin, he'll probably touch your dress, if only to take it off. Make sure it's pleasing to the touch.

Fabrics hold a resonance, an energy that can add to or detract from the message of your fragrance and color. Fabric sets the stage.

Fabrics by Type

- **Silk** This is a fabric of attraction. It can lend mystery to your look, because it veils you while being alluring. For instance, from behind silk you can create a strong magnet for attraction but reduce your vulnerability. Silk is fluid, protective, suggestive.
- **Wool** Has a more welcoming sort of appeal. It is very approachable and can give you a nurturing, earthy air. It gathers in energy, like a pair of open arms. Pay attention to the stiffness or fluidity of the material. It dramatically changes the message.
- **Cotton and Linen** These are the least sexual of the natural fabrics. They are more open, spacious, and light, which may be a good thing if you are feeling down or inhibited. It can also give you a sense of clarity. While you may opt for cotton for its comfort in warm weather, use color or scent to communicate your interest.
- **Damasks, Satins, and Velvets** While not "fabrics" per se, these are the passion raisers. Their richness invites touch and exudes warmth and heat. The sheen of satin and the glow of velvet signal open sensuality.
- **Leather and Suede** As one might immediately free

associate, leather implies power. Those dominatrices know what they're doing. Leather brings out the animal, the masculine lion. Conquest from the predator's side.

Suede still weighs in on the masculine side but is softer, tamer. Be aware that wearing either makes you a force to be reckoned with. Be sure you're in the mood to back it up.

- **Chiffon and Drapeables** Suggest and hint at what lies within (or under). They are the opposite end of the spectrum from leather and convey fragility. Wear it if you want to lean on shoulders and have your drinks fetched for you.
- **Man-made Fabrics** As you might imagine, man-made cloth has no personality nor any particular resonance. Here color, design and fragrance will carry the day.
- **Prints and Patterns** Strong patterns throw up a barrier without eliciting the desire to know what is behind the screen. This is not exactly conducive to attraction and seduction but great for business.

Combining colors in prints does not combine their powers but mutes their messages. For example, emerald, gold, and pink will not elicit a powerful, earthy virgin.

Here's an example of how a pattern can send a message. If you wear a herringbone sheath à la Audrey Hepburn, it is akin to being a walking fashion page from Vogue. You will be admired from a distance. Strong, confident, personal energy is key to pulling it off. Otherwise the outfit advertises itself and not you.

A woman wearing a leopard skin skirt may look like she's on the prowl, whether it's her intention or not. Make sure you wear the clothes and that the clothes don't wear you.

DELIGHTFUL DELECTABLES

Time for your just deserts. Your activities may first include eating, and, if this is the case, you can make the most of your oral fixations.

Here's a list of lust-inducing and passion killing edibles. As a rule of thumb, nuts and berries or fruits with seeds are generally good for some action. Just stay away from messy or processed foods, since they'll distract you or sap your energy. And be sure to use your lips and nibbles to suggest more personal activities.

Note there are no heavy foods like meats and oils. Keep at least part of your appetite for later!

BEWITCHING FOODS*

Lust Inducing

asparagus	chocolate	mint
avocado	cinnamon	nuts
caper	dill	olives
caraway	eggs	onion
carrot	endive	radish
cashews	garlic	sesame
celery	licorice	vanilla

*These can also be used as offerings in the rituals you'll be doing.

Love Inducing

apple
apricot
avocado
barley
beans (really!)
beets
brazil nut
cherry
chili pepper
coriander
figs
ginger
leek
lemon
lime
maple
papaya
peach
pear
peppermint
plums
poppy seeds
raspberries
rosemary
strawberry
thyme
tomato

Passion Killers

coconut
cucumber
fresh orange
lettuce
pineapple

ANCIENT FEMININE ROME

Heat shimmered off the tile floor as she walked along the interior courtyard of her villa. Her fingers ran along the chilled, smooth surface of its marble wall. She paused at the entrance of her bath to linger on a balcony overlooking the hills of Rome.

Next to her was a table laden with ropes of precious stones. Their sheen greatly pleased her and soon turquoise, coral, and jade cords were loosely wound about her throat. She noticed how well they matched the silvered rings he had brought back from the land of the pharaohs.

It pained her knowing her lover would not return from the wars for many months. She remembered their parting words, as they both understood that while their hearts belonged to each other, they would seek solace in another's embrace.

The bacchanalia tonight would provide a welcome diversion. She ran her fingers through her hair, as her consorts would later, while pressing their lips to her neck, her shoulder . . .

She untied her light cotton gown and it fell to the floor, pooling around her ankles. She stood naked, raising her arms to the radiant sunlight. Languidly she watched the orange blossoms and jasmine floating in the water. She sat on the edge of the brilliant mosaic tub and took off the heavy necklaces, swirling them in the water. The flowers danced on the ripples.

With a sigh, she slipped in. The heavy, silken water swirled around her, lapping at her skin like a thousand soft tongues. The oils of the flowers exuded their scent into the air and left lingering traces on her body. Later their powers of allure and seduction would help her attract a plethora of lovers.

A servant entered with towels of fine spun linen as she stepped from the bath. She stretched out on a divan. The servant returned to massage her back and thighs with rich oils. Gently aroused by his touch, she pretended he was one of the young men attending tonight. A shiver of anticipation ran down her spine.

As the shadows grew long in the courtyard, she rose to adorn herself for the evening. Selecting a flowing robe in deep terra-cotta and golden umber silks, she draped it over her body. Its colors would signal deep sensuality. With rubies for passion on her fingers and ears, she was ready to begin the night of erotic promise. But she was not yet done.

Into a glazed blue cup she poured the summer's first wine. And with the dates she'd gathered earlier from her garden, she presented them to Bacchus, god of lust and libation. She set flowers and oils before the goddess Venus, to attract and tempt the most interesting suitors. When all was beautifully arranged on the altar, she sat before the low table, breathed deeply, and meditated to open and heighten her senses.

She lit a candle and held it before her body. Its flame glowed before the centers that gave birth to her sexuality. She visualized them—the small central rotating circles below her navel and above her feminine sex—and felt the fire's warmth. Her breath pulled the flame's energy into her body to ignite her sensual powers.

She passed over the remaining five centers with the exception of her heart. Her hand rested between her breasts as she remembered the tenderness she had shared with him. Then, with great care, she shielded her heart with an agate pendant hung from coral beads. Thus her promise to him that no other would have her love as they took her body would be honored.

With her Inner Sight, she saw the coming evening filled with exceptional erotic delights.

TWO

Psychic Sex Appeal

You enter the festive atmosphere thinking, "Great, this party is filled with fabulous people."

Clad in an emerald green sheath, buoyed by the scent of patchouli, you're ready to begin bewitching. A sudden peal of feminine laughter captures your attention. You look in the direction of the sound. Your eyes alight on a new arrival, wearing a pale aquamarine dress and flowing peach scarf, holding court in the entryway.

Your defenses are up. You've followed all the instructions from this book down to the color of your toenails; she's only been here two minutes and already has three princes vying for her attention. What gives?

Understandably perplexed and perhaps a trifle irritated, you casually walk by and check her out. As you pass, you breathe in the fragrance of orange blossoms and musk.

You realize she's been reading this book, too.

But something still puzzles you: What is that extra ingredient, that special quality that makes her so magnetic? It is summed up in three words: PSYCHIC SEX APPEAL.

In ancient times, enchanting women were able to easily summon up their inner sex appeal. Like Cleopatra and Helen of Troy, they knew how to fine-tune their powers of attraction so that men dueled for their favors.

"Great, I'd enjoy turning the man in my life into a legendary lover," you say. "How exactly is it done? Do I color my hair? Change my toothpaste?"

Sorry, even with all the wonders of modern science, no product in this world can create a sexual allure that is more powerful then the one you already possess—that of being a woman. The sexual bewitchery tools of color, scent, etc., only provide a beautiful embellishment to your real charms:

Your true sex appeal lies in your psychic energy.

Surely you've had the experience of being "on"—you feel wonderful and the world seems filled with new promise. (Like when you're in the midst of a blossoming love affair, taking the baby for a stroll on a gentle spring day, or holding court at a business meeting.) Everyone, even your grumpy old boss (male or female), comments on how fabulous you look. Nothing's changed, physically you're still the same . . . except for your energy. As it shifts, people literally see you differently—more becoming, more light. With a little help and some practice, this wonderful feeling will no longer be left to chance.

We assure you that you are not a complete novice. After all, there is a little Helen of Troy in all of us. Vestiges can be found in your natural inclination for a luxurious, perfumed bath and playing mood music before a romantic rendezvous. These are energetic boosters that help conjure up an "I am fabulous" feeling.

What actually produces that special glow? **Your aura: the source of your personal energy and, of course, your psychic sex appeal.** It surrounds you every breathing moment and holds the power to touch people or repel them—whether you realize it or not.

To visualize it, picture a soft cloud of colored light all around your body. That's what your aura looks like. This energy is fluid and malleable. It shifts to reflect your physical and emotional states, and communicates that feeling to others.

If this is new to you, the following simple exercise will help you to sense your aura.

SENSING YOUR AURA

Hold your palm up to someone else's palm. Let your palms approach until they are roughly three to six inches apart. Keep your hands there, moving them back and forth, until you feel something—it might be heat, tingling, or a slight sensation of being pushed back. You are feeling someone else's aura.

For a more advanced exercise, each of you can try strengthening or diminishing the energy by concentrating on the force of the energy in your hand. Try to sense the aura as it changes.*

*For you skeptics, this is not body heat: Check out Kirylean photography. Auras do exist and can be physically captured on film. Some people can even see them.

It's normal to feel foolish or doubt yourself at first, but don't let that feeling get in the way. It is not just your imagination. This will be very important as we go on because for magic to materialize, you have to believe!

Did you ever meet someone and immediately "clicked"? Or shake someone's hand and feel an instant dislike? If you could sense the kind of person you were dealing with when you first met, it's an indication that you are tuned in to auras. You are feeling the other person's energy as it mingles with yours. When it's true love, you experience the power of two auras—his and yours—beating as one.

Auras extend beyond romance into other areas of life. For example, you know you are in the presence of someone powerful when you can feel his or her aura from a distance. The Dalai Lama has the ability to extend his energy to an entire crowd of people—and let each individual feel his compassion and love—just by shifting his aura.

The Seductive Aura: Your WEB

While you meld your aura to suit any situation, enchantresses find it a particularly useful tool for love and seduction. This requires putting a different, sexy spin on your energy that transforms your everyday aura into your seductive, alluring, embracing WEB, or Women's Energetic Body.

It is easy to see how useful this would be when you are in the mood for love. For instance, when you are attracted to someone, you instinctively charge up your aura to capture his attention. (You know this because you get nervous from the excess energy.) Just imagine the difference it will make when you start to weave a skillful WEB. A well-woven WEB will:

- Increase your magnetism
- Attract a consort
- Shape and change how other people see you
- Send messages of enticement to your lover
- Join with your lover's energy to heighten the experience and deepen your connection.

Cleaning the Space for Weaving Your WEB

(NO BROOMSTICKS REQUIRED)

You would never go to a party with unwashed hair and objectionable breath. And you should never go with a dirty WEB either. Like anything else, your aura can become dingy, low, or simply negative with the wear and tear of life. A cloudy aura can make you feel tired, unattractive, and dull—not especially conducive to magic raising. Since it's a little tricky to put your WEB through the spin cycle, here are a couple of suggestions.

Clearing your aura (and your WEB) is simple and should be done at least once a week. Following ancient wisdom, our techniques always require the use of natural objects. Here we'll use the power of the four elements—fire, earth, air, and water.

SALT

Taking a shower or bath with sea salt calls upon the elements of water and earth. The salt (earth) pulls out the negativity and the water flows through your aura, washing it. Together they carry the energetic tarnish away from you and down the drain—leaving you refreshed and able to let your aura shine.

CLEARING YOUR AURA

> Use natural, large crystal sea salt easily found at the grocery store. (We do not recommend Dead Sea salt because we've found that there can be a negative reaction to it.) Dissolve it into the water if you are taking a bath so you can soak in it. During either your bath or shower, rub the salt over your body. Pay particular attention to the center line of your torso, palms, feet, and anywhere else that feels like you need it.

SMUDGING

"Smudging," a Native American practice, will also purify your aura. "Smudge," the mystical all-purpose aura cleanser, is dried sage, often mixed with cedar or sweetgrass. *Note:* When burned, it does smell similar to marijuana.

Usually made in the form of a stick wrapped in string, it can be bought in New Age bookstores, through mail-order catalogs, bath shops, and some health-food stores.

It combines fire and air—fire releases the properties of the herbs (sage rids you of toxicity, cedar or sweetgrass replaces it with positive energy), and the smoke mixes it with your aura. As the smoke dissipates, your aura is cleansed.

CLEARING YOUR AURA II

Light the smudge stick and blow out the flame. As it smolders, wave the stick through the air around your body. Pay attention to the same areas as in the exercise above. Continue as long as feels necessary.

An extra added bonus: You will be clearing the room at the same time. Terrific for the office (do it when no one is around).

Weaving Your WEB

WEB Weaving can be used prior to an evening of seduction or simply to feel good. And don't worry about attracting people you can't get rid of; unlike a spider, you can choose who sticks to your WEB and who doesn't.

FOR BEGINNERS

1. Sit down.

2. Close your eyes.

3. Take deep relaxed breaths, until you feel open and at ease. If you are having difficulty, alternatively tighten and contract your muscles starting with your face and working down. Then focus on your breath and let everything else drop away.

4. Raise the energy you want to create in yourself by:

a. imagining something that helps you feel lighter, more attractive (vacation spots, good memories)
b. re-creating a feeling you had in the past
c. patterning the energy on another person whose qualities you like.

5. Breathe this feeling in and fill yourself with it. Use all of your senses—visual, taste, touch, hearing, smell. Make it as real as possible. You can use photos, music, scents, and souvenirs to help you.

6. When the feeling is as complete as you can make it, allow it to flow beyond your physical body, into your aura. Be in the experience. Without breaking the spell, slowly open your eyes. Take the experience with you into the day.

You have just spun your first WEB. Select music, fragrance, colors, clothing that expresses it—let yourself be intuitively drawn to what will enrich and enliven your new creation.

Don't be discouraged if it is not clear on the first or even the fifth attempt. Like getting reacquainted with an old friend, it takes time. Believe you can do it and you are half way there.

ALTERNATIVE WEB WEAVER

1. Put on music that you really love or something you think will help you feel flirtatious, sexy, and confident. (We use *Walk Like an Egyptian* for some of our WEB casting. New Age bookstores have other tapes that may help you loosen up.)

2. Move with the music, sing to it, let yourself go. You are the star. In this mood, with the music still playing, prepare for your day or evening. Note: It never hurts to wear something slinky or luxurious.

WEB *Maintenance*

Your invisible cloud of beauty and mystique wafts with you out the door and into the car but then . . . where did it go?

At first it may be difficult to hold your WEB in place for a long time. Practice and clearing will help and, while weaving your WEB, you can hold an object—preferably something made from natural material, like jewelry, a clear quartz crystal, or a silk scarf. (This is ideal since you can wear it afterward.) Your object takes on the energy of your WEB, which gives your WEB an anchor and helps you sustain it. It is easier to remember and reconjure a fading WEB with an anchor.

No two WEBs are alike. You can go naughty, innocent, regal, or just girl-next-door. Here are a few of the WEBs our friends have tried.

WEB #1

Sharon's WEB: *Innocent Allure*

This WEB is a wonderful way to begin your practice. It is easily handled and not likely to create negative energetic disturbances. Our friend Sharon was curious but timid about using her new-found abilities. We helped her to safely stir up some interest.

Sharon selected a weekend when she had nothing particular to do. We recommended she try her WEB at a museum where she could test it on people who did not know her.

Sharon wanted to liken her energy to Doris Day in *Pillow Talk*. Holding a pearl choker, the trademark of the fifties' feminine style, she breathed in the color pink, and the feelings of vivaciousness, freshness, innocence, and strong forthrightness. She wore a guise appropriate to her WEB: cotton sundress, the aforementioned pearls to anchor her WEB, hair brushed off to the side, and the fragrance of rose.

She went to the museum, alert for clues her WEB was up.

Results: Guards fell over themselves to help her, she could have sworn a young man was checking her out but she didn't encourage him (Doris Day wouldn't, after all), and on the way home someone told her she was like a breath of spring. Sharon swiftly progressed to more advanced WEBs.

WEB #2

Liza's WEB: *Compelling Allure*

If you are seeking a WEB to strengthen interest, intrigue, and passion, this is a page out of Delilah's book.

Liza requested a WEB to raise her current consort's fascination for her. On our advice, she arranged to meet him after work at a restaurant. (New and anonymous surroundings often help him see you in a new light.) This is the WEB she wove before meeting him.

Just after dusk, Liza sat before a table with a red candle and a pink rose in a beautiful vase. She lit the candle and then sat in a comfortable chair, dressed only in a silky bathrobe. Once she was relaxed, she put Madonna's *Vogue* on her stereo and turned up the volume until she felt it in her body. Taking the rose from its vase she danced around the room with it. Her movement raised her sensual WEB, she danced until she felt captivating and strong.

Staying in this mood, she perfumed her body with jasmine and got dressed, rose in hand. When she arrived at the restaurant, a bit late—on purpose—she kissed her consort with passion and brevity (Madonna style). She paused only to put the rose in his lapel and quickly left to seek the rest rooms.

In the bathroom, alone, she looked in the mirror, into her own eyes, and allowed the mystery and beauty of her own power to emerge. She returned to him with a calm and catlike demeanor.

Result? He suggested they order dinner in.

WEB #3

Faye's Stunning Allure

This is the modern woman's dilemma—how to gracefully encounter the new lover of your ex. Faye was facing exactly this. She was going to a party where she knew she would be seeing her former husband and his twenty-something girlfriend. Naturally her reaction was to try to make the girlfriend look bad. The old ways hold a different answer. Don't waste your time and power diminishing the other; make yourself shine instead.

Clearing was first on the agenda, all the anger and fear Faye was holding restricted her energy. We did not require sainthood, a little anger can add electricity if handled well. Then we recommended she make her body and self-esteem purr by indulging in a makeover—hair, nails, massage, etc.

The night of the party, purged and pampered, Faye gathered power objects: earrings her children had given her, an award she had received for her work, heirlooms from her strong grandmother, and a bowl filled with fruits (to represent feminine power and sensuality). One by one, she held them and allowed herself to feel the pride, power, and the accomplishment each object offered. As her WEB began to glow with the colors of her own strengths, she spoke these words aloud.

I acknowledge and honor
these gifts which are myself.
I weave them into my cloak of power.

Feet firmly on the ground, she imagined the power from the center of the earth flowing up into her legs, filling her body, connecting her with the ancient Goddess. Again she spoke:

Great Goddess and my source of light
I invoke your power in me tonight
From now and through the evening hours,
I claim and conjure my glorious powers.

She imagined herself at the party, dancing, laughing, and chatting, using her power. To finish, she ate a piece of fruit from the bowl and placed her palms on the floor to return the power of the ritual to the earth.

Faye called us shortly after the party, ecstatic. She'd had a fabulous time and an interesting new man she met had already phoned. She was also bemused by her complete disinterest in her ex-husband and his date, even though she noted with satisfaction that he followed her everywhere with his eyes.

She knew she had untangled her WEB from his. Faye now wears her power more easily.

Some Advice About Power Objects

- Each object should mean something to you personally.
- Any object you carry should be made from natural materials.
- Specific feminine power objects include: flowers, crystals and gems, bowls and vessels, shells, fruits, candles, water, and incense. Use any of these things as long as they feel positive to you. They can be things you associate with someone you love—such as an heirloom from your favorite great aunt.
- Stay away from things associated with painful memories or things you don't really like.

Basic WEB Weaving: Summary

While there is no exact formula (bewitching is highly personal), you can use this outline to imagine and create your own WEBs.

1. Clear your WEB first.
2. Gather any objects you need or want to use.
3. Sit quietly, preferably after dark, though with enough time to conjure before he gets there. (No rushing.) Turn off the phone and answering machine.
4. Be creative and comfortable; magic knows no limits.

WEB Weaving for Intermediate Bewitchery

To take your power to the heights of enchantment reach into your WEB's sources: the seven psychic sexual energy points on your body, also known as chakras. Yours are already working, you are just not conscious of it. Our ancestral sisters used their centers skillfully and constantly.

For those of you already familiar with chakras, here's a quick review with a sexual spin. If these sources are new to you, you're going to love them. Learning them won't be hard, either, since you're only relearning ancient knowledge; it's not like learning algebra.

Think of Salome dancing the Seven Veils. She opened and pulled back her centers, drawing in and rejecting prospective lovers.

Seven Sources for Sexual Bewitchery

Your centers are not visible to the naked eye; they are felt rather than seen. Your centers receive psychic energy from other people and transmit your psychic energy to others—it's a subliminal communication network.

They are often represented in artist's renderings and literature as rotating circles (like little whirlpools) which act as doorways to be opened or closed, bringing out or pulling back your powers.

These seven centers appear on both sides of your body, front and back. We are going to use them repeatedly throughout the book. (Part of that lost ancient wisdom we talked about.) They are the keys to deep sexual bewitchery.

Take the time to become completely familiar with all of them. Refer back to the descriptions and exercises whenever you feel you've lost touch. No one gets it all at once. Practice, faith and a little bit of magic will give you access to these powerful sources and your mystical side will come alive.

Center One (Root)

This center is easy to remember. Located at the pubic bone and base of the spine, above your sexual organs, the root generates the raw force of life and sex. The root center is the most connected to earth, a very feminine source of energy. If you imagine a cord traveling from the center of the earth to the base of your spine, you may feel your root center pulse.

Its dark red energy (which, if you visualize, may also help you to feel it) contains both desire and the physicality of sexuality. As you might imagine, this source is very important in sexual entrancement.

ROOT EXERCISE

Sit in a chair with your back straight, both feet on the floor. Breathe into your abdomen. Feel your legs and feet on the floor.

See if you can sense a connection with the ground through your feet. Feel the weight of your body and the gentle pull of gravity keeping you connected to the earth. Tune in to the base of your spine and see if you can feel a subtle current of energy running down your legs into the center of the earth. This is the root center.

Breathe into it, sense it within your body, visualize dark red filling this area. If you need to, place a cupped hand over it—whatever helps it come alive for you.

Can you feel an energy pulsing or turning in the area of your pubic bone and/or at the base of your spine? What is your impression of it? Does it change? Do you feel it has opened? Does it feel warm or hot?

Stay with it and breathe. You may also feel emotions or see images. Open to this experience and let it happen. No matter what your mind is telling you, there is no right or wrong way to do this.

Center Two (Navel)

The navel center is roughly two inches above your root, slightly below your belly button. When you are first attracted to someone, this center is aroused. Touching and nurturing will raise its powers. The desire to reproduce and mother, both feminine experiences, originates here.

This energy center is where emotions, pleasure, passionate connection, and personal desire are added to the more primal sexual urgency of the root. Softer by nature, its color, orange, is more mellow than that of the first center.

NAVEL CENTER EXERCISE

Place your hands over your navel center, just an inch or so beneath your belly button. Think about someone you're attracted to—a movie star, a lover, anyone who rouses your passions.

Breathe into this center and see if you can feel its

energy increase. Feel or visualize an orange light filling the center. Is it hot, warm, cool, difficult to feel, empty?

Keep breathing while you are doing this, resting your hands over it. Think about creating a child. How does this feel? Does it change?

Continue by shifting your focus to other people—lovers, parents, friends, siblings. Pay attention to any reactions.

Note: Your "gut instincts" come from this center.

Center Three (Solar Plexus)

The solar plexus waxes and wanes with your personal power; it is found at the central base of the rib cage. If you want to stand out and be noticed, activate the solar plexus center by "breathing" the color yellow into it. This is the center that rules your personal power and ego drive—your presentation of yourself to the world.

For the seductress this source is not terribly useful. Only when you are fighting with your lover, playing master/slave, or are in an unequal relationship is this center activated in sexual pursuits. Rape, an act of violence and power, would be experienced through this center.

SOLAR PLEXUS EXERCISE

Stand with feet planted firmly on the ground. Raise your arms above your head with your hands clasped together and your back slightly arched back. Stretch, breathe in, and, with a release of breath making an audible "Ah" sound, let your body swing down so that your arms go through your legs. Repeat this five to ten times.

Then stand and focus on your solar plexus. Breathe yellow light into it. See how it feels. (This is also an anger release, so if you are at all enraged, anticipate having a reaction.)

Center Four (Heart)

The heart center is summed up in a single word—*Love:* for him, for you, for life. The heart center, in the center of the chest, becomes expansive when you make love with someone you care about. Perhaps you have felt a warm glow here.

The green energy of the heart is the balance or midpoint of the seven centers. Also associated with this source is joy, grace, acceptance, and unconditional love. It differs from the second center in that the heart does not need to be stimulated by desire of someone or something. It is a state of being. You can use this center to help others and yourself feel more at ease.

HEART CENTER EXERCISE

Often the first thing that this exercise brings up is sadness—allow it to surface and dispel—it will make room for more happiness and serenity.

Place your fingertips on your heart center. This

spot, located between your breasts on the hard central bone of the chest, is often tender.

Gently press your center. How does it feel—physically, emotionally? Do you immediately think of someone or something?

Imagine yourself sitting inside your heart. Now breathe. Try to feel acceptance and love for yourself. Then fill the center with the color green. Is it a deep green? Is it light? Keep breathing. See if you sense the compassion and peace this center can bring. (This one may not be so easy, so give yourself some time to become familiar with the way it works.)

Center Five (Throat)

This source is the reason incantations release the power of magic. Groans of pleasure raise your ecstasy in lovemaking. From words of love to cries of passion, you express your desires and love through the throat center. Blue will give those expressions clarity.

However, the throat center is not just concerned with speaking, it is also about listening—taking in the expression of another. The energy of this center involves creativity, symbolism, and articulation of thoughts and feelings.

THROAT CENTER EXERCISE

Start with neck rolls, gently allowing your head to roll back and forth and around. Then tilt your chin slightly back. In long slow tones, recite the vowels, *a, e, i, o, u* several times. Be sure not to raise your shoulders.

Keep making a sound: Hum a tune, say whatever you want to, just make noise through your throat so you can feel the center working. Now send blue light into your throat and see if it changes the sound. Notice how the color or the sensation of the center shifts when you change your tone.

Center Six (Third Eye, Brow)

Unless you're actually with Richard Gere, this is the center you'll use to imagine being with him. Fantasy and imagination from this center will inspire you to new and exciting pleasures. We use this violet-colored center for fantasy and illusion, to embellish and to inspire our romantic reality. Sexual pleasure can be heightened when you use this center skillfully.

It is also called the third eye, which is a reference to its powers of insight and intuition.

BROW CENTER EXERCISE

Have a cool wash cloth handy. Close your eyes. Place the wash cloth on your forehead, covering the brow center, located just beneath the center of your forehead, between and above your eyebrows.

Breathe the color violet into your brow center. Feel the sensation on your skin. Remove the wash cloth and see if the sensation changes.

Send an image out from your brow center projecting it onto a "screen" in front of your eyes. Allow images to arise freely. Then breathe the "screen" back into your brow. Put your hands lightly on your forehead and rub this center in a counterclockwise direction.

Center Seven (Crown)

The crown center is located on the top of your head. When your lover is a puzzle, tune in to this spot to figure him out. In total sexual surrender, your energies will weave together all the way to the top—joining you as one. This center is white—all the colors combined.

At its most basic level, the crown represents comprehension and understanding. The understanding isn't just in the mind though, it also includes your connection to the "greater" spiritual consciousness, whether it is God, Buddha, Spirit, or whatever your preference may be. Like the root center, which connects you to the earth, this center has a cord that travels up to the heavens, keeping you tuned to a universal source. (Now if we could only learn to listen!)

CROWN CENTER EXERCISE

Sit with your legs crossed and back straight—as if you are suspended from a string. Breathe out through the top of your head, sending your breath upward to the ceiling or the sky if you are lucky enough to be outside. See if you can sense a connection with the heavens. Feel the weight of your body diminish. Tune in to the top of your head and see if you can feel a subtle current of energy running down into your body. It will probably feel light, expansive, and open. This is the crown center.

Breathe into it, sense it, and visualize the color white. Mingle your energy with the energy you are receiving from "all that is." Can you feel a pulsing sensation? What is your sense of it? Does it change? Is it open or closed, loose, rotating, fluid; does it vibrate? Stay with it and breathe.

Exercise addendum If you are having trouble with the centers, here are some tips.

- Wear the color of the center.
- Place or hold on the center a stone or gem whose color matches it. (Example: Ruby or garnet for the first. Topaz for the second. Amber or citrine for the third. Emerald or green tourmaline for the fourth. Sapphire or aquamarine for the fifth. Amethyst or fluorite for the sixth. Diamond for the seventh. Or the multipurpose clear quartz will work for any center.)
- Rub the center in a clockwise direction or cup your hand over it.
- Liberate your imagination, don't doubt what you feel, see, or hear. Believe in your intuition.
- Learn some meditation skills as meditation can help you in many ways: stress reduction, getting new ideas, going deeper into magic. These skills are easy to learn so check the appendix for guidance.
- Use scented oils to raise the power of each center. (See the list in the Seven Centers for the Sexual Sorceress on page 53.)

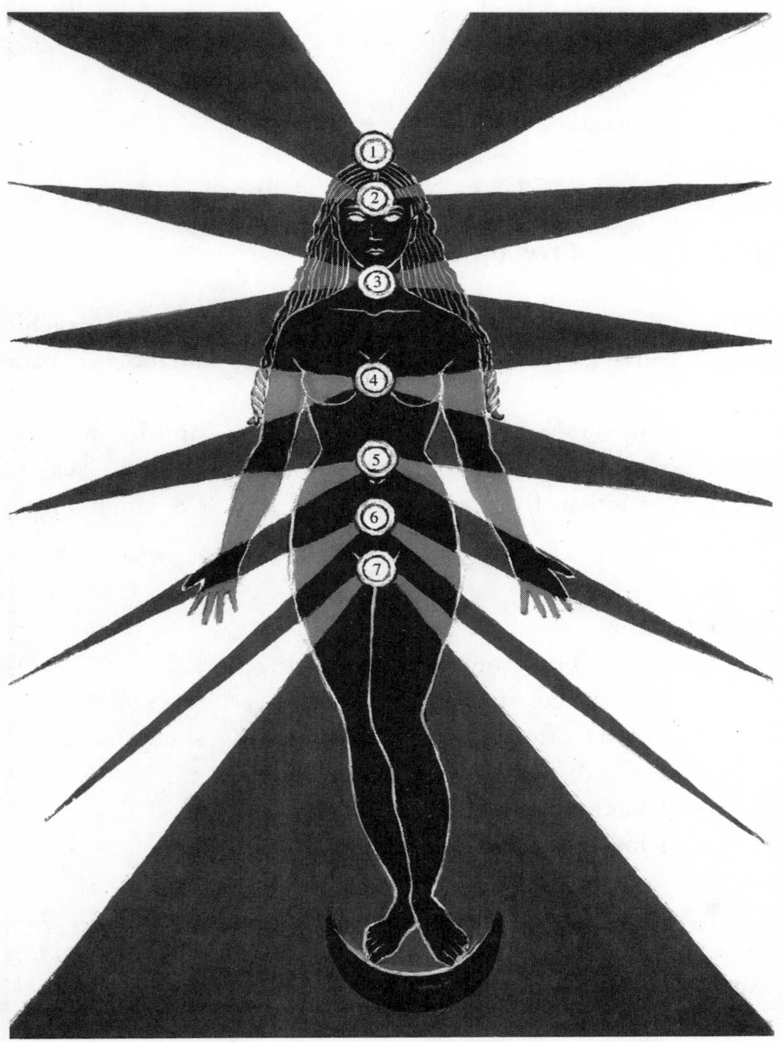

The Seven Centers

Try these with a friend so you can share experiences. It helps to have the support of someone else. (Yes, you are allowed to giggle.)

How Centered Are You? Find Your Source of Sorcery

Answer these questions and find out more about your psychic power centers. Work with your strengths and bolster your weaknesses.

Check all statements that are true for you. And by the way, don't expect to say yes to everything. (If you do say "yes" to all, you're either from another planet or on a mountaintop in Tibet.)

Root Center

1. I feel very grounded most of the time.
2. I often feel strong sexual urges.
3. I don't often feel threatened by the situations in my life.
4. I have a healthy body.
5. I love being in the country.

Navel Center

6. I express my emotions easily.
7. I consider myself emotionally flexible.
8. I love to pamper myself.
9. I consider myself a passionate woman.
10. I often find myself nurturing others.

Power Center

11. I'm not easily intimidated.
12. I have a strong will.
13. I have a lot of energy.
14. I achieve my goals.
15. I am comfortable with myself.

Heart Center

16. I have a positive outlook on life.
17. I can honestly say that I love myself.
18. I often feel compassion for others.
19. I have old friends.
20. I am able to sustain a long-term relationship with a man.

Throat Center

21. I consider myself a good communicator.
22. I don't mind voicing my opinion.
23. I like listening to other people.
24. I am not afraid to ask for what I want.
25. I have a lot of ideas.

Third Eye Center

26. I remember my dreams.
27. I get a lot of strong hunches.
28. I have an active imagination.
29. I am visually oriented.
30. I have experienced déjà vu more than once.

Crown Center

31. I am inventive.
32. I'm drawn to spending time alone to think or meditate.
33. I like exploring spirituality and/or the occult.
34. I analyze my motivations and reactions.
35. I like learning new things.

Your Power Sources

A "false" response to a question may indicate a weakness in that power center. Or, if you have a resounding "yes" to all the questions in one group, you have a struck a strong chord.

One way to double-check your answers is to summon the colors. That is, if you are strongly attracted to any of the colors associated with your sources that source is very comfortable for you. Conversely, if you have an aversion to a color, you are less connected to its source.

Power Center Colors

Root	Red/black
Navel	Orange
Power	Yellow
Heart	Green
Throat	Blue
Third Eye	Indigo/Purple
Crown	White

If you want to improve your energy in one or more centers, you can do so by wearing an outfit or a gemstone in its color. You can also pay particular attention to that center when you are clearing with smudge or salt.

This exercise will guide you through your sources, so you can bring their powers into your WEB.

You'll need fifteen minutes of uninterrupted quiet time for this exercise. To open the centers more deeply you can dab the following scents on their respective sources. (They are in order from bottom to top.)

1. Root—Jasmine
2. Navel—Ylang ylang
3. Solar plexus—Carnation
4. Heart—Rose
5. Throat—Lily of the Valley
6. Third eye—Lavender
7. Crown—Patchouli

Arousing Your Seven Powers

Sit with your back straight.

Clear your mind and breathe naturally. Let your body relax. (This will shortly become second nature.)

When you feel open and peaceful, imagine yourself in a lush, beautiful landscape. You are a daughter of ancient Egypt, dressed in white linen adorned with gold and turquoise. You walk over the lush fields of the Nile to the temple of the goddess Isis where you will await your lover. You call on her energy to help you ready yourself.

You breathe deeply into your first center at the base of your torso. It pulses with the deep red of embers, you fan the glowing coals. With its heat, your sexual urge begins to rise.

You remember your first meeting and the irresistible attraction between you. An orange glow in the center of your abdomen summons your desire for him and him alone. Thoughts of his touch, his smile, his strong body excite you and increase your passion.

With your hand on your solar plexus, you summon your powers. You know your strength is part of your appeal. Sending bright gold light causes the center to open. It gives you a confidence that he will later enjoy.

Tenderly, you feel the new love emerging between you. Its radiance fills you with joy. A soft green light emanates from the center of your chest, around your heart. Your reluctance to fall completely in love melts, you are ready to partake of love's pleasures.

You feel the amulet around your neck and whisper his name. You chant his name and yours together, and evoke the name of Isis to raise your sensuality. A sapphire blue light lends power to your voice.

You imagine your bodies entwined together. From the middle of your brow, you conjure his face before you. To better see your true love's energies, your center is opened by a violet spiral. The links between you are strong; you are assured of his love.

Finally you connect with the heavens and are drawn up out of your body. You skillfully breathe your energy back down to your root, the first center. Over and over you sense each center in turn until your WEB is aglow with love, passion, and desire.

Don't expect to see vivid colors the first time you try this, but don't be surprised if you feel a strong reaction later on. Often the impact of a meditation takes time to be felt. If any of your centers were murky or difficult to feel, go back to the preliminary exercise for that source or do a clearing.

There's a reason why it's called a practice. The more experience you have, the more skillful you will be and the better the results.

Even if don't think you are getting results at first, give the exercise a chance and you'll see things happen when the time is right. Magic works in mysterious ways.

Sex and the Seven Centers

Now that you have begun to skillfully manipulate your own WEB, you can start to weave it around as you please. (Never do it with force or negativity. We promise you won't like the results.) These practices are for you with your lover. He won't know what you're up to—he'll just feel it. (And we promise that he'll like it.)

If you've done your WEB work, you will be aglitter with sexual magnetism. Use the exercise Seven Centers for the Sexual Sorceress to shine forth, then try some of the following exercises for more direct enticements. Don't worry about doing any of these perfectly. You can change, modify, or forget a movement and still get results. This is playtime, after all, not work.

If you want some extra magical support, keep some lavender nearby, or drop some rose petals or dried orange peel around the area you'll be playing in. These are herbal boosts to keep you relaxed and on course.

You can also "charge" a crystal or any gemstone to help you with your energy. Just blow on it the way gamblers blow on dice while holding your intention in your heart and thinking about making love. Keep this stone nearby when you're in a seductive mode.

EXERCISE # 1 STROKING HIS AURA

If your consort has been oblivious of you, here's a way to rouse his interest.

Location: This can be done anywhere.

Tools: Red gemstone or jewelry he gave to you.

Lighting: Any light will do.

Wait until your consort is still, either sitting or lying down, even in front of the TV. (We hope it's not football—this is tough competition.)

Sit or lie next to him in a relaxed manner (not necessarily sexual). Hold either the piece of jewelry or the red gemstone to summon your passionate energy. With your other hand two to three inches over his heart center, make slight circles in the air, as if massaging him. This can be done from the back or the front.

If he asks you what you are doing, take no notice of his reaction, give him a slight smile, and continue.

As your hand hovers over his body, move it down to his root center (#1) and then back up again, caaressing his aura as if you are stroking a cat. Stop and stroke any center that draws your attention as you ascend. Repeat this three or four times.

Move your hand over his throat center (#5), stroking its energy a few times, then move on to the brow center (#6) and do the same. Don't go beyond the brow.

Go back to wherever your hand felt most comfortable, but be certain to return to centers #1, #2, and #4. Let your hand move naturally.

Don't forget to breathe into your centers, lest you forget your own passion while stirring his. Be sure to rouse your root.

Stay with it, stopping when it feels complete, be relaxed, and notice his reaction and your own. (Keep in mind that a reaction may not surface until later.)

You are just beginning to learn how to use your centers, and results are not important at this early stage.

Suggested Variations

- You can do this when he is sleeping, which is good for a first-time effort if you are shy. Don't be surprised if your consort is a bit frisky the next morning.
- Try sitting astride him and do it before you're about to make love. See where it leads.

EXERCISE #2 PRELIMINARY PASSION SURGE

Try this one to see a new height in the heat of the moment.

Location: Wherever you are making love.

Tools: Musk on center #1.

Lighting: Whatever you want.

Before you make love, dab musk onto your root center.

During the beginning stages of making love, when you are just starting to touch and kiss, open your energy centers. Breathe the energy from each center down to your root—you can also visualize the energy as a growing light if it helps. Brush the energy down to your root with your hand or take his hand and stroke it down your body.

Hold the energy in your first center until you feel it strongly—typified by heat, heaviness, physical sensation, and sexual arousal. It won't take long.

Feel his root energy, also. Men are easy to read; just feel his intention to make love. Open yourself to his energy.

At this stage you have two options.

1. You can send (mentally "seeing" it enter him) your root energy into his root before penetration; it feels like your body is swelling against his. This arouses both of you further before you join physically.

2. You can contain your root energy (feel it centered in your body) until he enters you, almost pulling your body away from his. It will release automatically when you join together.

This may cause a faster peak, greater pleasure, more passion for both of you. You can learn how it works best for you with practice.

EXERCISE # 3 THE KISS OF MAGIC

If you're a saucy sorceress, you'll find, share, and raise pleasure everywhere.

Guess what this one is about? Yes, it's time for one of your consort's favorite activities but perhaps it's not one of yours. Now you can make it a satisfying experience for both of you.

Location: Anywhere he can drop his pants.

Lighting: It's up to you.

Tools: Tongue-in-cheek.

Kiss your way down to his root, breathing energy from your root into each of his centers along the way, dawdling as you get closer to your final destination. (You can caress his penis occasionally if you like.)

When you get to his root center, take his penis in your hand gently, kissing and licking the tip. You can stroke it against your throat to connect your centers.

Pull the sensation and excitement of your root energy up into your throat, further connecting his root to you. It will heighten your pleasure significantly. Don't put his entire member into your mouth until your own root energy is aroused and you can feel it.

(If this act is uncomfortable for you, open your brow center and allow yourself to fantasize.)

Keep your root energy flowing into your throat and start to intensify your motions with your mouth and hands. Do what stimulates your own root—and don't be afraid to play with the areas surrounding his penis, including his thighs and testicles.

Use his rhythm to pace your motions and feel your power: You are in total control.

Keep the energy active in both your throat and your root until he releases or you move into intercourse.

Confidential to Reluctant Swallowers

This is a highly personal decision and does not increase or decrease the power of the experience. Do as you like.

SHE WALKS IN BEAUTY

She walks in beauty, like the night
Of cloudless climes and starry skies;
And all that's best of dark and bright
Meet in her aspect and her eyes:
Thus mellowed to that tender light
Which heaven to gaudy day denies.

One shade the more, one ray the less,
Had half impaired the nameless grace
Which waves in every raven tress,
Or softly lightens o'er her face;
Where thoughts serenely sweet express
How pure, how dear their dwelling-place.

And on that cheek, and o'er that brow,
So soft, so calm, yet eloquent,
The smiles that win, the tints that glow,
But tell of days in goodness spent,
A mind at peace with all below,
A heart whose love is innocent!

—GEORGE GORDON, LORD BYRON

THREE

Seduction: The Art of Ancient Feminine Wiles

It's time to learn how and when it's best to attract a new interest or reignite a current passion. But first we must dissolve some myths that stand between us and our seductive powers.

Myth Buster #1

Nice Women Don't Seduce

First to go is the ridiculous myth that female seductive powers are somehow linked to destruction. Starting with Eve, this theme runs through history with Salome, Mata Hari, even the Duchess of Windsor. It couldn't be more wrong. Feminine seduction is the power to entice and embrace, not the power to manipulate.

Face it, this is where we can have a lot of fun. When the element of risk is mixed with vulnerability, woven with power, and sprinkled with a dash of lust (and humor doesn't hurt, either), passions will fly.

What is seduction? Is it a path that leads inevitably to the bedroom? Good Goddess no!

Seduction is a dance of enticement and excitement, not just a warm-up to sex.

Seduction is paying attention to one man, opening yourself up to the pleasures of sensual play. It is an exploration of energies, and an excellent way to experiment with your powers. Lovemaking is not a foregone conclusion.

Myth Buster #2

Seduction Is Just for the Early Stages of a Relationship

Seduction should be a permanent part of your sensual repertoire. It is not just a means to attract someone. It's about keeping him, and yourself, interested and alive.

Our friend Lynn is a massage therapist at a spa. She works in casual clothes. But each Friday night, she arrives with a gym bag packed with a change of clothing and makeup.

One Friday, as Lynn left dressed in a flowing peach dress, the curious receptionist finally asked her why she went to all that trouble.

"After all," the hapless woman said, "it's only your husband you'll be seeing."

Lynn raised an eyebrow and replied, "I've learned it doesn't matter what you wear when you first fall in love with someone, the clothes never stay on for long. Remembering your feminine wiles and using them after the initial passion wears off keeps that excitement going."

We've heard she is often rewarded for her seductive savvy by finding her husband is waiting for her—a candlelit dinner on the table.

Myth Buster #3

Seduction Is Just for Him

If you look and feel good about yourself, you will be sexier and more seductive. We hope the bewitching tips you've tried have already raised your appreciation of this. Once seduction is a part of your life, you are in the flow of your own feminine energy—which is fulfilling, enhancing, and otherwise enjoyable. This power spills over into other areas in your life and makes it more satisfying and creative.

Now that we've dispelled the myths you're free to seduce without restraints. Let's turn from talk to action. . . .

Ready, Set . . . Seduce?

Having the hots for a consort, whether he's a new conquest or a current beau, doesn't mean it's time to start casting your WEB.

First, consider how you'll feel if he does not respond, or worse yet, turns you down. Not because there's much of a chance your charms won't be noticed, but because it's a good barometer of how likely it is you might trip over yourself.

For example, if you are so intent on the outcome of your

efforts, he may be blown away by your intensity, not your passion, and run for the hills.

If a rejection will turn you into a puddle, this fear may keep your powers in check and your seduction will frizzle instead of sizzle.

Before enticing a consort, you need to be confident within yourself. Whether or not he succumbs to your magic, there'll be no question in your mind that you are fabulous. After all, there's always another day and . . . another man.

If the idea of playing seductress makes you nervous, stop right here and go back to Chapter 1 and review Bewitching Arts and Techniques. When you get more comfortable using your BAT, your seductions are sure to take flight.

In short, the only wrong time for seduction is when one of you isn't up to it.

Tuning in to His Station of Love

Before you start summoning your powers, it helps to be aware of your consort's preferences. Your bewitching will be far more successful if you know how he likes to be approached. For example—

- Is he aggressive or shy?
- Will it be day or night?
- Will you be alone or among others?
- Is he intellectual? Sensual? Down to earth?

And, most important,

Is he available?

We want to remind you that being a temptress does not entitle you to pluck whatever prize you wish from the masculine world. We believe that if he's attached, he's not up for grabs.

This is the first rule of magic—call it the Karmic Golden Rule. Do unto your sisters as you would have them do unto you. Whatever you put out, you get back. Is he worth the risk of losing your love one day to a similarly sticky-fingered sorceress?

Once you've looked in the cards, or at least at his ring finger, and found him to be available, you'll want to make sure that your overture will appeal to him. Champagne and soft music may put you in the mood, but maybe a mountain hike is his idea of romance. Look to the heavens and find out more.

All you need is just one basic piece of information—his birthday. You don't need the year, just the date. Be clever about it—ask him, not directly of course, but with some flair.

Our friend Marie always says, "I hate having my birthday in the middle of winter. Are you lucky enough to have yours in the summer?" This is usually enough to get the information. If he just says "no" and walks away, think twice about him. It may be a signal from the universe that this fellow is not for you. Learn to listen, it saves a lot of time and pain.

Once you know his birthday, figure out his astrological sign and the element it is associated with. The twelve zodiac signs are divided among fire, earth, air, and water. Each responds to different enticements. Getting to know his element can help guide your seduction to a fabulous conclusion.

Fire	**Earth**	**Air**	**Water**
Aries	Taurus	Gemini	Cancer
3/20–4/19	4/20–5/19	5/20–6/20	6/21–7/21
Leo	Virgo	Libra	Scorpio
7/22–8/21	8/22–9/21	9/22–10/21	10/22–11/21
Sagittarius	Capricorn	Aquarius	Pisces
11/22–12/20	12/21–1/19	1/20–2/19	2/20–3/19

It's Elemental, My Dear

Fire

This is a passionate, volatile element, with a lot of energy. Fire signs like action for the sake of action. Success is not always important. Fire signs move on to new ventures with ease. The warrior nature of Aries, the royal behavior of Leo, and the adventure-seeking Sagittarian typify this energy. Men born under these signs are likely to be action heroes in their own minds and react best to scenes out of *Raiders of the Lost Ark*.

Examples

Alec Baldwin (Aries)
Antonio Banderas (Leo)
Denzel Washington (Sagittarius)

To Appeal to the Fire Man

Light up his element with candlelight or firelight.
Dress-up can include props, wigs, and costumes.
Play intriguing, passion-inspiring music.
Concoct surprises of any kind.
Focus totally on him.
Whisper suggestively.
Touch him passionately all over his body.

Earth

Earth signs are more interested in physical reality than adventure. They like nice homes, beautiful things, and steadiness. More stable than the fire boys, home-loving Taureans, practical Virgos, and ambitious Capricorns are equated with material goals, luxury, and riches.

Examples

George Clooney (Taurus)
Hugh Grant (Virgo)
Mel Gibson (Capricorn)

To Appeal to the Earth Man

Display art, beautiful things, flowers and plants in your home.

Show off your pets.

Wear or use lush fabrics, including velvet, satin, or fur.

Use cushions and comfortable furniture.

Serve well-prepared food, especially something made by you.

Keep surprises to a minimum and focus on creating a relaxed, cozy atmosphere.

Use music to deepen the mood.

Enjoy tactile pursuits like back rubs, holding, and hugging.

Air

The element of air is chatty, curious, and thoughtful. Air can be heavy with storms or light with breezes. Expect mood changes in the signs of effervescent Gemini, balanced Libra, and eccentric Aquarius. If you have an air man, interesting conversations, ideas, and reading materials can feed his inquisitive mind and bring him closer to you.

Examples

Liam Neeson (Gemini)
Will Smith (Libra)
Tom Selleck (Aquarius)

To Appeal to the Air Man

Surround him with his element by burning incense and wearing perfume.
Display good books (only those you have read) and conversation pieces (photographs, unusual souvenirs, collectibles, etc.).
Ask him questions (and listen attentively to his answers).
Set a light mood with music.
Suggest going to plays, movies, theater.
Inspire intelligent conversation and humor.
Focus on lips and kissing.

Water

Water is the element of emotions: deep, sensitive, and enigmatic. It is a complicated element—transforming itself at will into liquid, solid, or gas. The intuitive water signs of Cancer, Scorpio, and Pisces are wounded by sharp words, and telling a lie to one is a fate worse than death. Nurture and cuddle these sensitive creatures.

Examples

Sylvestor Stallone (Cancer)
Lyle Lovett (Scorpio)
David Duchovny (Pisces)

To Appeal to the Water Man

Offer him a bath or libations: wine, tea, water, etc.

Consideration of any magnitude that will show you care.

Let him choose the music.

Snuggle together in small, cozy "safe" spaces.

Use slow and languid movements and savoring touches.

Massage his feet, hands, and head.

Elemental Seduction Stories

A Fiery Meeting

Caroline had been trying to catch Paul's eye for a long time. They worked at the same pharmaceutical company in different departments but had several friends in common. A Halloween costume party given by a mutual friend allowed Caroline her first chance to put Paul under her spell. Discovering his birthday from a company list, she knew right away how to use Paul's Aries fire energy to her advantage.

She arrived at the Halloween party with a Morticialike wig covering her dark blond curly hair. Heavy makeup, red lips, and a beauty mark made her look unusually exotic. She wore a long black sleeveless chiffon dress with a red silk scarf and high heels. She put aside her loathing of press-on nails and sported long red claws that she used to beckon and gesture.

For a half an hour she played the vamp to the obvious enthusiasm of many men. Buoyed by her success, she made a beeline for Paul as he walked in. Caroline surreptitiously slipped in her vampire fangs and greeted him from behind with a neck nibble. She was surprised by her own brazen behavior—but Paul's reaction was even more satisfying. He took her in his arms and bent her back, giving her a long, Hollywood-style kiss on the lips.

Caroline pretended to swoon and enjoyed his laughter as he caught her. He hadn't recognized her and spent the next fifteen minutes trying to ferret out her name. Taking her cue from his keen interest, she played coy and fed his curiosity, eventually unveiling herself as his co-worker. All night, she played the role of seductress, arousing interest from many quarters and making sure to drift by Paul from time to time.

At the end of the evening, Paul drove her home, and left her with a kiss that suggested more to come.

An Earthy Seduction

Amy knew exactly what she wanted—Brad, a Taurus. Understanding the Taurean love of comfort and beauty, she decided to use them to her advantage.

Amy asked him to read a draft of her thesis and invited him over to her apartment to discuss it. Though a novice to enchantments she easily managed to conjure up a sensual yet homey atmosphere to appeal to the earth man.

Amy wove her WEB the night before. She lit a red candle and, holding a plant with pink flowers in her lap, she breathed into her root and her heart center. She imagined herself connecting with Brad in a relaxed, sensual manner. The plant found a convenient home in the kitchen window to anchor her intention and WEB.

The next day, Amy greeted Brad wearing a cropped coral silk tee-shirt and faded low-slung jeans, no shoes. She wore a light gold chain around her neck. Her hair was up in a casual knot. In short, she was a vision of earthly delights.

Brad gave her a shy, appreciative smile and allowed himself to be led into the kitchen, where warm, freshly baked cookies and brewed coffee awaited him. With a satisfied sigh, he relaxed into a chair with mug and manuscript in hand.

Amy silently slid some cookies in front of him and put her hands on the back of his chair as he started to read. She leaned over his shoulder to see his notes on the paper, allowing her gold chain to brush against his shoulder.

Later, while they discussed her paper, Amy subtly communicated her interest by bending toward him. As he spoke, she took down her hair and shook it out. By the time Brad left, they had made a date for dinner and a soft, lingering kiss at the door gave Amy his response to her seduction.

An Air of Attraction

After several dates, Claire and Lawrence had not even kissed yet. Frustrated, Claire wondered if his being a friend of her brother's was holding him back. She found him very attractive and wanted to shift him out of her fantasies and into her arms. It was time to take action.

Lawrence shared her brother's birthday, making him an Aquarian. Deducing they might be attracted to similar pursuits, she used her brother's devotion to Sunday morning news shows and the weekend crossword as the keys to her plan—a cozy, intimate Sunday afternoon, with room for more. . . .

Lawrence arrived at Claire's place, happy to see his favorite news show on the TV. Claire placed the Sunday papers within his reach and busied herself in the kitchen.

She returned with mimosas and sat next to him on the couch. They chatted during the commercial breaks, with Claire leaving from time to time to finish her brunch preparations. Finally they sat down to eat. Claire left the TV turned down but not off. This mistake made conversation difficult as Lawrence's eyes constantly wandered to the flickering screen. He complimented her on her soufflé and finished off the champagne, Claire suggested they'd be more comfortable on the sofa. She asked him questions about the show, trying to create a more intimate connection.

As the show took over his attention, Claire excused herself to clean the dishes, and returned to find Lawrence fast asleep. Oops.

Remember using his element should help you turn his thoughts to your tantalizing self, not *Meet the Press*. Make sure sensuality is the focus; for example, a soft whisper is a better use of the air element. Keep things simple. (During their next meeting, Claire used music and a book of poetry on one Friday evening. The results were much more to her satisfaction.)

Sea of Love

Teresa wanted to give Henry, her Scorpio husband, a memorable fortieth birthday. Knowing he disliked parties, she secretly booked a mountain cabin where she planned an evening of intimate reconnection.

The room overlooked a lake lined with pine trees and came

complete with hot tub. She arranged to have their favorite cognac, a basket of delicacies perfect for a cozy dinner, and a humidor of his favorite cigars delivered to the room. In her lingerie bag she slipped a small bottle of massage oil scented with bayberry for use later in the evening.

Henry complained when she packed him into the car. (He, like many Scorpios, hates surprises, but sometimes it is worth it to go against their natural inclinations.) He quickly settled down when they arrived at their small mountain retreat set in its spectacular scenery.

One look at the hot tub, massage oil, caviar, and cognac, and Henry happily surrendered for the rest of the night. It has become a much anticipated annual event.

The above stories are a sampling of the many ways to summon the element of your intended and lend its potency to your seductive magic. Obviously, they, like any enchantment, are not meant to be formulas. There's nothing worse than stale sorcery. They are also not guarantees for success, but they do help. Learn from mistakes but don't give up. Let your intuition guide you and remember to make it pleasurable for yourself as well.

Timed to Perfection

Before you rush out and plan your next elemental seduction, check the calendar. What day of the week is it? What season is it? What cycle is the moon in?

Though it may seem like a lot of bother at first, every good enchantress learns the importance of the mood nature sets and uses it to her advantage. Follow these easy spellbinding basics to create timely seductions.

Days of the Week

Each day of the week is ruled by a different planet. This knowledge predates ancient Greece and helps in planning special evenings—and avoiding disasters.

Day	Planet	Evoked Qualities
Monday	Moon	Emotional, internal
Tuesday	Mars	Feisty, aggressive, masculine
Wednesday	Mercury	Communicative, versatile, restless
Thursday	Jupiter	Spontaneous, extravagant
Friday	Venus	Beautiful, harmonious, romantic
Saturday	Saturn	Restrained, practical, structured
Sunday	Sun	Creative, restful, spritual

What days do you think are best for seduction? The safest day of the week is Friday, ruled by Venus, the planet in charge of love and relationships. Its energy embraces sensual quests and encourages happy endings.

Though Friday has a special mystical kick, all the days of the week have something special to offer. After all variety adds spice to love as well as life. Use this list as a guide.

Monday Good day for cozy intimacy, simple pleasures, and no surprises.

Tuesday Brings warlike Mars into the boudoir for fiery, passionate couplings. (A little bodice ripping anyone?)

Wednesday Light and communicative Mercury makes it wonderful for first dates, witty repartee, and whispering sweet seductions in his ear.

Thursday Jupiter's expansion leads to daring. Try out a new outfit, go somewhere different, take a new plunge.

Friday Venus smiles on any kind of romance and love to bring the heartfelt side of seduction to fruition.

Saturday Saturn turns things on the heavy side so it is certainly not our favorite day. It is unfortunate, given the work week, that this is the most convenient day for dalliance. So if you're going for it, make sure that you are both rested. Take a nap. Organize it well, and don't do too much—it's not a good day for overloading.

Sunday The biblical day of rest, and not a good day to set off new sparks. However, this is a great day to loll in bed and see what happens when you've already made some progress.

Moon Cycles

The moon's cycle marks off more than just your menstrual cycle. Whether moonlight is growing brighter or receding, you can use it for your bewitching powers.

The waxing moon grows bigger, building from zero to full. The light swells, making it a juicier, more abundant time. This is good for heading into uncharted territory, like seducing someone new or trying out a new look.

The day of the new moon marks the beginning of this cycle. (Check your newspaper for this date.) It is a deeply feminine time, excellent to conjure up a WEB or to summon anything you wish to create in the next month. Partake of the powers the new moon offers—they are truly magical.

When the moon reaches its apogee, it is full. This is a wild, magical time, but also unpredictable. So while you should enjoy the spirit of the full moon, don't necessarily rely on its illusions to hold true. Seemingly solid decisions often melt into flights of fancy. The man who is fascinated by you tonight may be gone tomorrow.

The full moon's light dims slowly over two weeks. This is called the waning moon, a time of decreasing energy. Become more intimate with your consort. Plan cozy modes of seduction. If you try to do anything bold during this time it will take more effort because you are working against the natural flow.

Seasons for Seduction

Seasons affect everyone's mood with their special beauty and themes. Keep them in mind when you select a motif for your seduction. You don't have to follow these suggestions to the letter, but trying to force devil-may-care summer fun into a snuggle-in-front-of-the-fire winter evening will require working against nature.

Winter This internal season suggests mellow, slow, dark, intimate, and cozy.

> *Colors:* Jewel tones, metallics, black, and white
> *Feelings:* Fear, insecurity, dreamy, meditative

Spring The time for growth suggests an unfurling, a new birth; being frisky, rejuvenated, and resurrected.

Colors: Soft pastels, vibrant greens
Feelings: Anger, passion, vitality, active

Summer This time of year brings movements that are languid, still, sensual, lazy, hot, ripe, and hedonistic.

Colors: Hot orange-based colors (pink or tomato red), bright green, purples
Feelings: Joy, satisfaction, abandonment, casual

Autumn When the leaves turn, thoughts of the bountiful harvest, and the winding down of the year take over, suggesting melancholy, transition, and reflection.

Colors: Earth tones, russet, copper, deep yellow
Feelings: Grief, releasing/letting go, gratitude

Pop Quiz

Test your seductive prowess. Select which element(s)—fire, earth, air, or water—best matches the following activities:

1. Taking a walk
2. Having a drink at home
3. Having a drink at a bar
4. Going to an auction
5. Going to a play
6. Antiquing
7. Going to a roller derby
8. Staying in bed all day
9. Going ice skating
10. Going to a flower show
11. Attending a lecture
12. Hiking

13. Spending two-plus hours kissing
14. Lolling in a bathtub
15. Taking a sauna
16. Reading all day
17. Dancing
18. Surprising them
19. Taking a class together
20. Bungee jumping
21. Cooking
22. Grocery shopping
23. Having no plans
24. Making love

Answers

1. All
2. Water, Earth
3. Fire, Air
4. Earth
5. Air
6. Earth, Fire
7. Fire
8. Earth, Water
9. Air, Water
10. Earth
11. Air
12. Earth, Air
13. Everyone at the beginning of a relationship
14. Water
15. Fire, Water
16. Air
17. Fire
18. Fire
19. Air
20. Fire
21. Earth
22. Earth
23. Earth, Water, Fire
24. Everyone

Don't worry about how many of these items you got right. This quiz is just a good way to get used to associating different activities with different elements, as well as giving you ideas about what your elemental man might like to do.

S Is *for* Seduction

Think, for a moment, of a man seducing a woman. He "sweeps her off of her feet," going after her with relentless drive.

Now think of a woman doing the same thing to a man. Not a pretty sight. Women are generally more potent using a weaving, feminine flow of energy, indirectly attracting their lovers. We call this approach the *S* move.

It is easy to learn because you already do it unconsciously when you are attracted to someone. It is the turn of the head, the lowering of the eyes, a sigh, your shoulder curling in. It is a natural part of being a woman.

Unhappily, we have noticed that the survival of the *S* move has become endangered ever since it was unjustly considered too passive for the "modern woman." (Somehow women got into competition with men and started using more masculine, direct approaches.)

It is not a sign of weakness or subservience to weave your energy around a man. It is feminine, appealing, safe, and part of the dance of seduction. It's curious that our favorite seductress was in her prime earlier in this century. We're talking about the celebrated sex goddess, Mae West.

A Salute to Mae

"It is better to be looked over than to be overlooked."

—*Mae West*

If you feel hopelessly separated from your feminine seductive powers, rent a film and watch the expert, Mae West. Her voice, her movements, her gestures make her an inspiring role model. She was not afraid of her own sexuality or what anyone else thought of it. She was a strong person and powerfully feminine.

The Many Faces of Feminine Wiles

Mae is only one of many seductresses who can inspire you. Below we have listed some of our favorite personas a woman can use to attract a man. Imagine yourself in the role to see how it feels.

Cinema Sirens

Indirect but in control: Kathleen Turner in *Body Heat*
Unconscious earthy sensuality: Sophia Loren in *Houseboat*
Unconscious sex kitten: Marilyn Monroe in *Seven Year Itch*
Ice queen: Linda Fiorentino in *The Last Seduction*
Innocent charm: Meg Ryan in *When Harry Met Sally*
Direct hit: Sharon Stone in *Basic Instinct*
Cool and arch: Lauren Bacall in *Key Largo*
Vixen: Vivian Leigh in *Gone with the Wind*
Young and innocent: Julia Roberts in *Pretty Woman*

Before You Seduce: The Ultimate Seduction Checklist

Prior to practicing your seductive appeal, review the basic Bewitching Arts and Techniques.

- Clear yourself with salt or smudge.
- Light a red candle, perhaps have flowers nearby.
- Bathe in a warm tub with incense or have a scented candle burning nearby.

- Perfume your body with one of the following oils: Cinnamon (sparingly), gardenia, jasmine, musk, rose.
- Wear a freshly cleaned garment made (if possible) of a natural fabric, preferably silk, velvet, or damask.
- Try earth tones or jewel tones and avoid strong prints.
- Wear garnets, opals, diamonds, deep flashing stones, or stones with fire.

Gather your enchantress energy by sitting or reclining before your candle and:

- Take in the persona you want to portray.
- Visualize the evening (or day) ahead of you.
- Remember to connect with your root energy center.
- Breathe into your root to open it.

If you want to take your bewitchery up a notch or two and surround yourself with some powerful feminine energy, recite these words:

Passions rising day or night,
Join with me in this delight.
Stars and moon and Goddess smiles,
Bring to me ancient feminine wiles.

Before you walk out your door or let him in, have something in the color red to carry or wear—a scented red handkerchief, a red ribbon (we like this tied on our wrist), or even red underwear. And remember, seduction is fun and playful—there is no goal except to enjoy yourself.

The "Party" Seduction

Use this when you want to entice someone while there are others around. It uses the art of subtle suggestion, barely visible to the eye, felt but not seen. Whether or not you know the man in question—it is a very alluring, safe, effective way to have him realize how much he wants to be with you.

First things first: We don't want you to waste time if he's not interested in you. Assess his receptivity with this easy test.

TESTING THE WATERS

Project a thought about your attractiveness to him, send your image to him, imagine making love to him when you are standing close to him. Pretend you are silently communicating to him. Then check for a response. Do you have a sense he is interested, a sense of connection? Did he leave the room? Do you feel like this will take a lot of effort? Use your intuition to see if he is open to you. And, toughest of all, be honest.

If he seems to welcome your psychic suggestions, carry on with your bewitchment. The following list of seductive sleights of hand will guide you.

1. Whether you are standing alone or with others, use your hand to gesture in his direction (fan yourself, toss your hair, or as a way of expressing yourself when you talk), softly send your energy and intention to him. Don't look like you are waving a tomahawk. This can be done intermittently.

2. When you have an opportunity, breathe in as you send your energy to him and let go as you breathe out. This pulls him to you, then suddenly releases him.

3. You can play by physically moving closer and farther away—to the same effect as number 2.

4. After you feel comfortable and psychically attuned to him, you may approach him (use your *S* move).

5. Once you are talking, show your interest in him through your eyes, posture, and body language.

6. When you are close to each other, feel the energy tingling on your lips. Don't send out your root energy here; keep it low key.

7. Use your whole body; move into his aura and away—the ultimate *S* move.

At this point, if he doesn't go for your lips or your phone number, just turn around. There'll be a line of men behind you dying to be noticed.

A note on subtlety We are going to bore you to death with this message: *Less is more.* Do not clonk the guy on the head with your message—nothing turns a man off faster than a clutching bewitcher. (If she still deserves that name.) Even if he wants to be with you, feeling pressured to "deliver" something will make him uneasy. And men love to feel there is a challenge, something to conquer. Maintain your aura of mystery, and you will bring him to your side and have him thinking he seduced you.

The "Home Alone" Seduction

When alone with someone and you have sex in mind, start with The Party Seduction but continue with step 8.

> **8.** Send your energy into his root through your hand, feel as if there is a soft beam of light or heat radiating between you. This doesn't have to be very strong and, after practice, does not require much focus—you can even do it with a drink in your hand.
>
> If you touch him (not on his root please! or not yet anyway), do it very lightly.
>
> Continue until you feel a tingling or warmth in your hand. Then open your own root center by breathing into it and wait for him to make a move.
>
> When he touches, kisses, leans up against, or otherwise signals his interest, connect your root and navel center to his. Enjoy.

After you've known someone awhile, you can use the direct approach. Men do like this as a change of pace, but not as an introduction.

FOUR

Mystical Sex Tips

In this chapter you'll learn to commingle your energies with your consort's to heighten pleasure and make magical love.

Elements of Love Revisited

Your seduction was a rousing success. He's at your feet, kissing your toes and you're more than ready to move on. And you say he's an earth man? A fire guy? An airy fellow? A water sport?

True, you already know his elemental makeup.

But what happens when your stars mix with his? It's important to know how to combine your energies harmoniously. That way you won't try to make the earth move and the waves crash only to be up to your knees in mud.

Elemental Combos

Look up your own sign and find your element. Now check out how your elements mix. If you're concerned that your magazine horoscope constantly tells you that you and your mate are astrologically challenged, don't worry. The sun is only one of many planets that influence love. The moon, Venus, Mars, and Jupiter all play a role. There are infinite astrological combinations that bring people together.

Fire–Fire Yikes! Fire feeds fire but can get out of control. Watch how your energies work together to avoid going up in smoke.

You both love the thrill of the chase, adventuring and winning—which can present a dilemma when you're after each other. Take some time to enjoy being together as a team as well as two enticing individuals. Otherwise your big flame may burn out too quickly.

Fire–Earth As long as you don't spark into a raging forest fire, you get along famously. Fire warms the earth and earth feeds fire. You can both gain from the energy you create together.

If you're the earth sign, you have a natural ability to calm him down. Use your stability and practical nature to steady his perpetual motion.

If you're the fire sign, you'll need to sit still and "smell the roses" a bit more than usual. But your earth man will also love your energy and spontaneity, too. You can blend your elements well.

Fire–Air Fire feeds on the oxygen air provides and air rises when warmed. So this is a good combination, as long as it doesn't get out of control, and you go up, up, and away.

Whether the woman is the air or fire sign, she usually talks or thinks a lot and listens little and may have problems sitting still. Ditto for him. Here's the trick: you're both really interesting people, but you need to take turns being quiet in order to appreciate each other.

Fire–Water Traditionally, this combo makes steam. If you can manage a balance and you both contribute evenly, you'll be fine.

If you're the water sign, remember that he doesn't crave the nurturing and sensuality you do, so you have to communicate your needs to him (without whining!). Too much water puts fire out.

If you're the fire sign, your sense of adventure and impulse may distract you while he's sitting there waiting to be cuddled. His depth can be just as intriguing, but ignore him and he'll dry up.

Earth–Earth You're both very grounded and enjoy tactile and visual pleasures, so your own instincts about what gives you both pleasure are probably right. Just watch out for routine and practicality, which can cause a dreadful rut. Variation is your friend. Remember sex needs energy and motion for the earth to move.

Earth–Air You can either kick up dust or create a very fertile, sensual playground. Air likes earth's consistency and earth likes air's ticklish changeability.

If you're the earth sign, you will learn a lot about communication from this dude. He is a talker, an idea man, and a guy who just likes to shoot the breeze. Most earthy women don't go in for idle chat, so use your quiet countenance to evoke mystery. He'll go wild with curiosity.

If you're the air sign, enjoy the steadiness this consort brings you. You can feel stable and secure (and that's very sexy) when you're with him. Try not to expect him to talk a lot or to use words to express himself. He wants you to feel his interest, physically.

Earth–Water Okay, this combination can turn to mud, but that's only if you're stuck. Otherwise, this elemental mix can bring a fertile but low-key joining, languorous rather than vigorous.

Whether you are water or earth you are an enigma of sensuality for your man. He'll love your urge to touch and feel. And you are both likely to be very sexually responsive, the ideal team for sexual bewitchery practices.

Air–Air You two could float away if you both exert your airiness in tandem. Like fire with air, your energy moves out of your body and into action. Sometimes this is good for love-making, but more often it creates distance, whether through dreaminess, talking, or just thinking about different things. Make sure you take turns focusing on each other, and for mysterious, sensual pleasure, tune in to the sound of silence as you seduce him.

Air–Water Mists, clouds, evaporation, and humidity are created by these two elements.

If you're the air sign, allow your clarity and self-expression to sink into this intuitive man. He'll be delighted by your take on his world. Just remember to hold him tight when you whisper your thoughts into his ear.

If you're the water sign, don't let his constant need to vocalize or intellectualize disturb you. Your soothing, deep water energy will calm him down, and you can use your intuition and sensual skills to still his mind and move his heart.

If either of you are under stress, you won't communicate well. Move carefully when you're fogged in.

Water–Water You two have a veritable ocean of feeling, sensuality, and connection.

You are intuitively connected, so you don't need too much help to know what he likes. Water signs also have a lot of sensual potential and can enjoy a very satisfying physical and emotional time together.

Waters tend to run deep, however, and you could both dive into your own worlds or dark sides. Keep afloat with communication, even when it's hard. Use touch and kindness to pave the way to reconnection and smooth sailing.

The Psychic Power of Sex

Sex connects you and your lover in very powerful ways. As you deepen your physical connection, so deepens your psychic bond and your emotional attachment. A friend of ours says that if women were more conscious of their psychic connections with men, bad relationships would end much sooner.

Your centers carry the memory of every consort with whom you have joined. See Chapter 7, Troubleshooting for Relationships, to free yourself of unwanted past connections.

When you are exploring sexual play with your consort, don't go beyond your own comfort level. There's a big difference between being adventurous and being an idiot. If you find it difficult to breathe and feel your body or energy tighten or withdraw, stop and think again.

Never, ever, just give. This can lead to obsession, an unequal relationship, and you can set yourself up for being used. Consult Chapter 7 if this pertains to you.

Basic-Lusty-Heartfelt Sex: Take Your Pick

Before you create your magical roll in the hay, we'd like to remind you there are different forms of sex. Each with its own energy and intention. Three immediately spring to mind.

1. Basic mating
2. Lusty sex
3. Heartfelt sex

Basic Mating

During this mode of coupling we seek to satisfy primal sexual urges without necessarily being too worried about those of our consort. You might think of this as the "regular" sex that long-term couples intersperse with heart sex and lusty sex. It is the time when we witchy women simply want a man, whether or not he is Mr. Right. Like the night you slept with the guy from the company softball team.

Basic sex has more to do with your aura than specific energy centers. It is a way of releasing both psychic and sexual—not necessarily emotional—charges. It shakes out your energy leaving you more tranquil and centered.

It works with your root center, which craves to be satisfied from time to time. Basic sex keeps it open and active so you stay rooted in your sexual self.

However, "meat and potato" sex does not have to be ho-hum sex. You can fire your powers to make even basic sex better. Movement and connecting with your centers is very important. To start you on your way, we suggest you try some of these root-raising exercises.

Exercises for Bewitching Sex

Root Stoking

You can use this exercise before you go out on the prowl or before you start having sex. It gives you extra root energy.

Stoking enhances basic sex by opening the root and

raising your interest level—and by the way, it helps tone your butt, too.

Breathing deepens the effect and will carry you into a deeper, more orgasmic feeling.

Lie on the floor with your knees bent, feet on the floor. Relax, then tighten all your pelvic muscles (butt, abdominals, etc.). You tighten as you breathe in and simultaneously curl your lower back so that your bottom is slightly off the floor (no more than a few inches). Exhale and relax. Continue to undulate your pelvis up and down until you sense the energy building in your lower body. You can increase the force and rhythm as you wish. Repeat as needed.

THE BREATH OF PASSION

This is an alternative root raiser and can be done along with the previous exercise or on its own.

Sit up straight, breathe in deeply, using your abdomen, and breathe out very quickly through your mouth. Make a hissing sound on your exhale. Do this for about fifteen seconds, and then draw in one last deep breath, hold it in, and then release it slowly, sending the warmth you feel into your root. You can increase the length of time, but if the room starts to spin, you're not reaching nirvana, you're just hyperventilating!

Lusty Sex

This is the kind of sex we yearn to have for ourselves, as depicted in movies like *9½ Weeks*. Lusty sex is that heart-palpitating, sweat-provoking, root magnifying, glue-yourself-to-the-guy's-body passion fest.

It is impossible to maintain this level of intensity all the time—don't even try because you're doomed to failure. This rush happens in the beginning of a relationship, can be sparked by that frisky feeling when you ovulate, when you're rejoining with your lover after a separation, when you view or read erotic material, and at other, blissful, unpredictable moments.

If you've just gotta have him and find yourself looking through your drawers for lingerie and perfumes, you're on the lusty trail. Grab your ruby (or garnet), put on some sexy music, and conjure up an atmosphere of seduction.

Lusty sex involves the lower three energy centers: your root, navel, and the solar plexus. The addition of the solar plexus is what turns you into a tigress. So scent them, open them, and revel in their energies. *No exercises necessary here, just let it fly.*

Heartfelt Sex

Haven't we been talking about this all along? Not really. This lovemaking is entirely different from either basic or lusty sex, although lust and love are a great combo. Heartfelt sex truly is the physical expression of love between you and your man.

Lovemaking engages your heart center and sends its energy to your lover. Your love can be tender, funny, compassionate, and most important, honest. Heartfelt sex involves all of your centers and, hopefully, all of his. You weave yourselves together, the heart and body joining as one. This is not always automatic. Here's an example.

Meg had been dating Christopher for three months and was nervous about their new sex life. She thought at first her skittishness was caused by her four-year-old son being in the next room, but the boy now stayed most weekends with his father, and nothing had changed. Meg was becoming insecure about her sexual skills and wanted to know more about using bewitching techniques.

From our discussion with her, we knew that her seduction skills were fine and, because she meditated regularly, we knew she was in tune with her energy centers. We suspected that a reluctance to be vulnerable was at the root of her fears. Meg and Christopher were a water-earth combination, so we encouraged her to use those elements to create an atmosphere where they could unwind and reveal new parts of themselves.

To ease her insecurity, Meg invoked the earthly goddess qualities of Gaia, and the flowing powers of Astarte. She donned a rose-colored silk sheath to attract Christopher and still feel protected. She dabbed musk on her root and heart to signal her readiness, and before Christopher arrived, she did the root pulse exercise (page 101) to kindle her own passion.

To bring the elements into her small bedroom, she placed a large silver bowl of water on her bedroom table. Pink roses and carnations floated on its surface, adding their properties of love, power, and protection. On a windowsill, a bowl overflowed with fruits and nuts. Draped over her bedroom lamps were sheer scarves in soft, warm colors, scented with cedar. A favorite Mozart string quartet played in the living room and gently permeated the bedroom.

A glowing Meg met Christopher at the door. He remarked

that she looked different—softer and more relaxed. He opened the wine he had brought and, noting Meg's attire, suggested they stay in. They chatted and sipped the wine, which Meg reported as having an excellent, calming effect.

Christopher reached behind Meg to turn off the lights as he began to nuzzle her neck. In the lowered light, the warm glow coming from the bedroom caught his attention.

Meg breathed energy into her root and smiled. He led her to the bedroom. Thrilled to find an atmosphere so welcoming to his advances, he drew her close and gave her a lingering kiss. They made love slowly that night, opening to each other in a way they hadn't before.

Meg surrendered to their lovemaking without reservation and even made a second overture to Christopher, proving her passion-raising skills were intact.

After this success, Meg decided she would continue exploring both her bewitching techniques and Goddess-raising energies.

Goodness of the Goddesses

There are many goddesses from ancient cultures all over the world. Their images and myths symbolize all the different aspects of femininity, whether it be mother, defender, protector, virgin, or seductress. As a woman, you can ask any goddess to come to your aid. Just call their names and they will lend you their wisdom and power. There's a goddess for every occasion, far more than we're able to mention. Just to get you started, here's a list of the kinds of qualities you might be looking for and the goddesses who can get you there.

The Glory of the Goddess

Feeling a little overwhelmed? Need some support? Just call on the heavens. You'll immediately be hooked up to a very powerful and ancient source. You can summon the goddesses to deepen your power, get over rough spots, and generally improve your craft.

Use their names during your WEB weavings, atmospheres, and lovemaking to add another dimension. Consult the following list and select the goddess(es) of your choice appropriate to the occasion. We do suggest, however, selecting two or three that you will use most often. Like any good relationship, it grows over time. For more in-depth information, see Appendix B.

Quality or Power	Goddess
Air rituals	Hathor, Wadjet
Body Image	Pele, Xochiquetzal, Aphrodite
Charisma	Rhiannon, Lakshmi
Childbirth	Anahita, Artemis
Courage	Artemis, Athene, Macha, Innana/Ishtar
Communication	Hathor, Athene
Compassion	Isis, Gaia, Innana/Ishtar
Conflict	Sekhmet, Wadjet, Artemis
Dancing	Ushas
Dating	Aphrodite, Lakshmi
Earth rituals	Gaia, Hera, Demeter
Earthly delights	Bastet, Gaia
Feline energy	Cybele, Bastet
Femine wisdom	Estsanatlehi, Innana/Ishtar, Brigid, Hecate, Athene
Fertility	Estsanatlehi, Macha, Gaia
Fiery rituals	Hestia, Pele

Flirting	Rhiannon, Hathor, Lakshmi
Growth	Cybele, Hera
His participation	Aeval
Home protection	Guanyin, Hestia
Home loving	Hera, Hestia
Love	Astarte, Cybele, Isis, Aphrodite
Lust	Aphrodite, Innana/Ishtar
Magic	Sekhmet, Isis, Hecate
Magical settings	Estsanatlehi
Marriage	Isis, Hera, Ushas
Music	Sarasvati, Bastet
Mystery	Lakshmi, Ushas
Optimism	Guanyin
Orgasms	Isis, Innana/Ishtar
Passion	Aphrodite, Hestia, Pele
Pleasure-seeking	Xochiquetzal, Ushas
Power	Wadjet, Cybele, Brigid
Protection	Anahita
Releasing the past	Anahita
Sagesse	Estsanatlehi, Ushas
Seduction	Macha, Hecate, Aphrodite, Sarasvati, Ushas
Sensual pursuits	Xochiquetzal, Sarasvati
Serenity	Athene, Astarte
Sex	Aphrodite, Isis, Anahita, Aeval
Sincerity	Hathor
Surrender	Artemis, Innana/Ishtar
Transformation	Isis, Estsanatlehi
Untamed abandonment	Artemis
Virgin	Artemis, Athene
Watery pursuits	Astarte, Benten, Sarasvati
Woman power	All goddesses
Working women	Athene

Joining with the Goddess: Your Orgasmic Source

An orgasm is a grand rush of energy—a physical, psychic, emotional release. It is one of the most pleasurable, profound and spiritual moments we have—by ourselves or with another.

The orgasm is born in the root center. To increase orgasm, weave your root energy back and forth into his during intercourse. With experience you can open and connect your other centers. The overwhelming energy of the orgasm rises through your centers and his. They may open one at a time or simultaneously. In fact, an orgasm can set off a spontaneous mutual explosion.

You can change which centers you open and see how it affects orgasm. Consider keeping track of your experiences in a journal to remember what creates spellbinding sex for you and for him.

Tapping Your Sexual Beat

Every woman has her own sensual rhythm, which shifts and changes. It's like your breathing, if you pay attention to it, you'll notice that it changes depending on what you're doing. Different days, different lovers, different acts of lovemaking will vary your ecstasy.

If you can't find your natural rhythm, be sure to keep in touch with your seven sources—they'll help you feel it. This is especially helpful if you get distracted during lovemaking and don't know how to reconnect.

As you become accustomed to working with your energy, let it flow. Experiment constantly with your consort—play with his rhythms and let him feel yours. Being in tune with yourself will help you have a richer lovemaking experience and keep you and him aligned.

EXERCISE TO RAISE YOUR PULSE

Pulsing uses your rhythm to shape your lovemaking sessions. During intercourse, use the motion of root stoking and imagine the energy of your root expanding out and drawing in with it. Pull him in and push him away, opening and closing your root physically and psychically. This will boost your pleasure and feed his fire by creating a cycle of energy between the two of you.

To focus on him, open your root and feel his pulse then shift yours to match it. If you want to guide him into your rhythm, concentrate more on your own, which will attune him. Doing the WEB wrap at the end of this chapter also helps.

Have times of nonmovement to just enjoy the sensation of being filled. You can use your perineum to tighten around him. Lust is often roused at a slower tempo.

Five Basic Positions for Scintillating Sex

1. Feminine over Masculine (You on Top)

If you don't know this position, it's time for a new adventure. It is your chance to be in charge. This is an excellent position for you to discover your rhythm and gauge the strength of your root energy. Play with him, chat, nibble, and massage, align your energy centers and take yourselves to the top.

2. Masculine over Feminine (Him on Top)

A pillow under your bottom or tilting your pelvis will help you maximize your connection. He's in charge here and you follow his lead, but naturally we have tips on how to be influential. Open your root and pulse it with a rhythm that suits you. This is a good position to connect with your heart center, which can add another layer of fulfillment.

3. Spoon or Feminine=Masculine (Side by Side)

This one needs no magic wands. As you lie on your side in front of your consort, wrapped in his embrace, you can add to your pleasure with your own hands to guide him. Practice opening your centers from the back. It is a good time for a more intimate, slow movement.

Cradling each other encourages a very deep root connection, especially if you move your body forward and arch your pelvis back to him. You may use this position when you want to introduce more tenderness into your lovemaking.

4. From Behind (on Your Knees)

Usually associated with lusty sex, this position has a very animalistic quality that can bring out your savage side. Use it to unleash wildness. This can add passion and spontaneity to your connection with your consort, leading to more imaginative situations.

5. Seated and Facing Each Other

We love this one, especially in a candlelit, scented bath. You can hold each other, with your energy centers almost touching. He is usually in control, but it is easy to find a rhythm that suits both of you. You can use this position to practice weaving your energies together, which creates a wonderful connection, joining on the physical, emotional, and spiritual levels.

There are so many other positions that we dare not go on since we'd never get to anything else. So see suggested reading for other books you can use to add to this knowledge. Explore. Experiment. Enjoy!

THE WEB WRAP

Natalie used this in our basic booster example. During lovemaking, wrap your psychic energy around his, forming a cocoon that cradles you both and intensifies your connection. It works best with basic or heartfelt sex, but can be used in lusty sex to lure him into your mood.

Try this alone first to get accustomed to it.

Increase the size of your energetic body (your WEB) by first feeling your WEB in the two or three inches of air surrounding your body. Then breathe and expand it into a "cloud" of energy beyond your skin. You won't be increasing your body size but you will have the sensation of being larger.

Just before or during intercourse, enlarge your WEB. As you join together, envelop his body with it, forming a private sensual space in which you both mingle and merge.

The WEB Wrap enhances the feeling of being as one. It can help if you or he feels distant or disconnected as well as boosting the energy and making it easier to stay in rhythm with each other. You can also use this just to cuddle and feel close.

Awake, O north wind;
And come, thou south;
Blow upon my garden,
That the spices thereof may flow out.
Let my beloved come into his garden,
And eat his precious fruits.

—SONG OF SONGS, 4:16

FIVE

Advanced Mystical Sex Tips

Now it's time to tell him that you are a practicing sexual sorceress. Don't panic. We'll help you break it to him gently. In our collective experience, this news is often very provocative—in a positive way. But we also understand that your consort may be a little skittish around the magic arts since it makes you knowledgeable in a way he is not.

One indirect method of floating the idea past him is to say that "a friend of yours" is using this book. If he is interested, you have your answer.

If you prefer a subtle but direct message, here are a few suggestions:

- Rent the *Witches of Eastwick* and ask if he wants to play Jack Nicholson's role.
- Say you "need to talk" about something. He'll be so relieved it's not about something he did, he'll love this.
- Leave the book by your nightstand and see what he says.

Tell him any way you want but don't set him up and don't push; in general, men don't respond well to pressure.

Once your consort has agreed, buy some flowers, light some candles, and try these three easy exercises together. Under your tender guidance he'll get the hang of it very quickly.

Bridgit had no idea how effective her skills had become . . .

Introduce Him to the Seven Sources

Sit comfortably with your consort and ask him to close his eyes. Tell him to breathe deeply as you describe the location and color of each center in a soft, low voice. Ask him to feel his seven centers, one at a time starting with the root. You can gently touch each one, too.

Try to open your own centers as you speak to him. You may find that this will immediately create a passionate reaction. Needless to say, this is a great warm-up to sex.

When Two Beat as One: Mutual Pulsing

Like your heart, your source and root energy has a beat. Your beat naturally affects your consort's—and vice versa—as you make love. If your beats are in sync, it will feel good. If not, it feels like you're out of step. The key is to use your root center and feel the rhythm you create together. We call this mutual pulsing.

Remember back in Chapter 4 when you used "root stoking" to rev up basic sex? Well this is the same thing *à deux*. Use a thrusting, rolling motion through your pelvis to open your root and, as he responds to you, he will be doing the same. Let the movement lead you to a rhythm that suits the two of you.

Pulsing can be done before or during sex. Find a pulse that is good for both of you, then play with it—faster, slower. Try containing it. Holding it back will prolong the experience, making it excruciatingly good.

Weaving

This is one way for you both to actively feel the connection between your seven sources. As always, you may want to use candlelight or scents to make an atmosphere conducive to magic.

As you make love, each of you consciously breathes from

your center into your partner's, starting at the root. Work your way up the seven centers to the crown. Then rejoin your energies at the root. You can stop after one cycle or repeat it as you wish. Feel the joining of your energy centers as you make love, and see how different the experience becomes.

When you are feeling comfortable with your sources, try this exercise to raise intimate feelings. (It can easily be done without him knowing it, too.)

SPOON MAGIC

You are behind your lover, who is lying on his side.

Kiss your consort's energy centers from the back, starting just above his buttocks, going up to the small of his back, base and center of his rib cage, nape of his neck, back and top of his head. Blow energy and color into each. This is also an excellent way to teach him where they are. You can also anoint each spot with scented oils.

Lie in a spoon position, behind your man. Then close your eyes and see your WEB, lightly encompassing him, your energies weaving together, front to back and back to front. Send energy to him from your centers, with particular attention to the first, second, and fourth. Accept his into yours.

Start to move your bodies together following the energy. It is like a dance. Your hands will naturally begin to caress him.

Experience the rhythm together. Guide his hands over his body with yours.

We suggest that the release come without intercourse. After the man's ejaculation, you take his place and he kisses your centers, spooning you the way you were with him.

If you want to have intercourse with this, we suggest that you be in front first, which will fuel the passion of your foreplay.

Advanced Mystical Sex Tips in Action

Now that you are practiced with most of the mystical basics, we hope that they are becoming second nature. You have, at your fingertips, a bewitching wardrobe; scents; colors and candles; an understanding of the qualities of fire, earth, air, and water; and most important, your WEB and use of your seven centers.

As you probably know by now, a lot of sexual bewitchery is up to you and your imagination. We'd like to share some examples of how our fellow bewitching practitioners have used their feminine wiles and hope they inspire you to create your own. Advanced Mystical Sex Tips illustrate the infinite possibilities that can be created by your powers. Lovemaking is organic and has little to do with position or form and much more to do with imagination, playfulness, mystical knowledge, and your own sensual self.

Belinda's Touch Technique

"I love the sensation of touch. For me it is the best way to get to know a man and to feel comfortable with him. I set my scene with candles and incense and use rich fabrics to drape over myself so that I feel like a sensual package ready to be unwrapped. I always leave a little suggestion of my breast to arouse his imagination. At this stage he's usually still dressed, which seems to be a terrific turn on.

"As he starts to disrobe me, I guide his caresses to the places I like best. Typically we take brief pauses while he eagerly undresses. But I always make him keep his shirt on. As we kiss and touch, I keep the pace slow and easy. I have him lie on his back and wrap his legs in my fabrics. Then I unbutton his shirt and kiss each energy center, starting from the crown and ending with a light kiss on his obviously inspired root.

"Now is his turn to guide me. I touch and caress him according to his wishes and lightly dab vanilla oil on his heart. From there, we move to a sexual galaxy all our own."

Woman of the Mists

"My lover and I are both water signs and these techniques inspired me to play with our element. One day while he was watching the football game, I went into our small bathroom and ran a very hot shower and closed the door so that steam would fill the room.

"Then, in our bedroom, I dressed in a sheer nightgown and braided my hair. I lit scented candles, and, upon taking them into the bathroom, I let a cloud of steam escape. I adjusted the temperature of the shower and got in.

"I heard his voice call after me *What are you doing in there?* So I invited him in. The sight of me with my sheer negligee clinging to my body created an impulse he could not resist. He stripped and joined me.

"I soaped him as the candles flickered in the misty room. It was like another world. He couldn't stop caressing me and touching me through the fabric. Finally he pulled up the gown while pressing me against the tiled wall. We slowly sank onto the floor of the shower, sitting under our homemade waterfall, enveloped in the mist, kissing lustily. With my third eye I imagined I was in a tropical forest and sent this image to him. We started to make love passionately.

"He just loved it. Next time I want to use cushions and bring him into my fantasy with tapes of jungle music."

Olivia's Lair

Olivia's husband had been asking her to take the lead in their lovemaking for a while. She had a penchant to try something a little wilder but didn't want it to be too direct. The seven source meditation from Chapter 2 gave her access to her ancient wisdom, and an image of a wildcat came to her. Since she loved cats, she knew this was a sign. Olivia consulted her newspaper for the date of the full moon and chose this time of potency to reveal herself.

Olivia prepared for her seduction by shaving all body hair and anointing her seven centers with musk. She sleeked back her hair and manicured her nails into a clawlike look. Black leggings, a tight black top, and a leopard print scarf tied around her hips made her feel positively feline.

She transformed her bedroom into a dimly lit, scented lair, covering the bed with a soft blanket. We'll let Olivia tell you the rest.

"He came home from work and I was curled up like a cat on the couch in the living room. He entered the room and I yawned, arched my back, gave him a look through slitted eyes and curled up again. He sat down next to me and asked me what was wrong. I snuggled into his lap and connected our root centers. After a few kittenish moments, I lightly clawed his face and slunk out of the room. I'd put some scotch and a glass on the coffee table so he poured himself a drink. This gave me time to light candles and hide in our bedroom.

"He came in looking for me, then turned and spotted me behind the door. I knocked the drink out of his hand and pushed him onto the bed. We tussled.

"I bit his ear and whispered 'Is this what you had in mind?' Before he could answer, I kissed him hard and nipped his lips, feeling his erection at the same time.

"He recovered himself and pulled me underneath him, pinning me down with one hand. To lull him into a sense of false security I began to purr. He relaxed his hold for a minute. I slipped away, into the other room, and stripped off my top. I tried to run past him but he caught me and threw me onto the sofa and undressed me. He barely had time to unzip his fly, he was so excited!

"We had wild sex on the couch. I used the root pulse to bring him into my rhythm. Now, when I'm in the mood, all I have to do is purr."

Ed and Nancy's Bacchanalia

Ed and Nancy take turns doing this one, so they each get a chance to direct the fantasy. Theirs are all about indulgence, adoration, lust, and earthy pleasures.

For Ed's enjoyment, they pile cushions before the fireplace and throw a satin sheet over them to make a free-form bed. There are a lot of candles—purple, white, and red—all around. Cognac rests nearby, with a bunch of grapes. The fire is lit before they begin.

Nancy dresses like a Roman prostitute: a lot of makeup, long hair (she uses a wig), and a sheer sheet of chiffon draped casually over her naked body. She trims and scents her pubic hair and puts a temporary tattoo in the crease of her thigh.

Ed, in a robe, lies before the fire. Nancy enters bearing a tray of oils and jars. Opera music plays in the background. She kneels silently before him and slowly opens his robe. They never speak. She anoints his centers with oils and massages his torso, then sits astride him. He gestures for the grapes. She feeds him slowly until he refuses her. Nancy then turns her back to him and chants over his root in a low voice. She administers the "Kiss of Magic" but stops short of his release.

Turning over to allow him a view of her root, she caresses herself as if to beckon his entry. He takes her from behind, and she hisses the breath of passion as he cries out from pleasure. They share a snifter of cognac afterward.

The bedroom is Nancy's favorite domain. A canopy of muslin creates a soft den. Fresh sheets lie untucked on the bed. Chocolate, flowers, and champagne are within reach. Pastel-colored candles scent the room with jasmine. A tape with sounds of the sea plays over and over.

She wears a completely see-through negligee, with pearls and jewels flowing down her body and in her hair. She is fresh from a warm bath and wears a jasmine scent.

Ed enters when she calls him, shirtless and wearing only jeans. He approaches the bed. She asks for champagne. As she sips it, he massages her feet, kissing them, and praising her beauty. He kisses and caresses her whole body, sending his energy into her centers, calling her his goddess.

Ed makes love to her very slowly. He lifts her negligee, fondling her breasts and body. He kisses her, holds her, and tells her he loves her. Nancy moves his hand down to her root, and guides it to her rhythm. She climaxes quickly.

They share champagne and chocolates until she is ready to begin again.

He kisses his way down her body until he reaches her root, where he teases and arouses her. She pulls his head back up and kisses him. He lies on top of her, matching center upon center, and breathes in deeply, exhaling his energy into her.

He enters her gently and rolls onto his back. Nancy moves in her own rhythm, pulling his energy into her to prolong the experience. They climax together and lie entangled in the sheets. She drowses as he strokes her hair.

Further Inspirations for Advanced Mystical Sex

Student/teacher
Cavewoman, caveman
The hunter and the hunted
Coquette
Adam and Eve (original sex)
The stranger
Love slave
Tarts and vicars
Spies
Vestal virgin
Doctor
Policeman
Lord/Lady of the manor
Rock star
Kidnapped/abducted
Dominatrix
Geisha
Harem

Obviously, you can take your bewitchery into many situations, even with more than one partner at a time. Your skills can be adapted into any permutation or combination you might fancy.

More on Accoutrements

Fruits
Liqueurs
Sex toys
Spreadables (cream, honey)
Paints
Feathers
Underwear
Fabrics of all kinds
Scented body oils
Bondage (ribbons, silk ties)
Videos, erotic literature
Mirrors
Yoga, Tantric sex
Sexy talk

If some of these suggestions make you pause, or if you have a fantasy that makes you feel slightly inhibited, consider using the full moon as Olivia did to help you unleash your energy. After all, lunacy is a term that came from the strange and improbable behavior people exhibit while under the influence of the full moon.

If the moon isn't full, you can also try going outside and breathing in the night sky. This can make you feel lighter and that all things are possible. Just don't stay out there too long, or you'll have a hard time coming back.

SIX

Mystical Troubleshooting: How to Unhex Sex

The highly skilled enchantress is never bored or boring. Even when her consort has a bit of trouble raising the magic, she knows just what to do. You can create the energy for continuous sensual play, longer-lasting experiences, and dealing skillfully with any problems that might arise.

Your bewitching skills are excellent for averting a crisis while it's still a small problem. Just keep your sense of compassion and humor (we do) when dealing with the snafus of sex and watch them disappear.

Enchanted Troubleshooting

If you are experiencing problems that relate directly to sex, there are simple things you can do to bring back the fire. And just to remind you this isn't a matter of life and death, we'll share a little levity along the way.

Comforting Your Consort

Wobbling Willies: Arousal and Delivery Problems

If your consort has consistent problems acquiring an erection (and it's not caused by alcohol, depression, or fatigue), he's probably just anxious. You can approach both the emotional and physical problems with your magic. But, whatever you do, dismiss your inclination to go to the source of the matter. Plainly stated: **Do not connect to his root!**

First, sweep his aura with your hand, removing any energy that you feel may be weighing him down.

Send him energy through your heart into his—i.e., unconditional love.

Do something relaxing, like giving him a massage, taking a hot bath together (use sea salt to help clear any negativity). Say you only feel like being close to him. And when you are cuddling, you can send root energy into him through your hand.

This is not a question of success or failure. It is a question of healing. Bear in mind that his anxiety can be contagious; use your magic to lighten the load. Be sure you are not attached to proving your powers as that puts too much pressure on both of you.

If problems continue, he should see a doctor.

It Was a Flop: Erection Dejections

Another common problem is an unsustained erection during lovemaking. (This often happens when men use condoms.) Gentle handling and encouragement can help, but if it won't come back, panic, fatigue, or disinterest has set in. Take a break and do something else that is intimate but not sexual.

We suggest a WEB wrap, where you send your aura around him to soothe and calm him, and bring you together as a couple so he won't feel alone. You can use the spoon position to make this easier.

Call in your favorite goddess and move along with her energy. You can also send him some root energy after a break (when he's not thinking about it anymore).

If this happens often, one of you isn't connecting. See rejoining.

Minute Men: He's Come and Gone

There are times when consorts come quickly and that's just the way it is. It's possible that you were simply too hot, especially if there's been a fabulous seduction and great foreplay. Give him recovery time and hope he'll gear up and do it again. (See The Second Coming in this chapter for more.)

However, if this is a constant problem, you can try a few root-soothing techniques to help shift this behavior.

Try to lower your root energy and divert his attention. Rub

your fingers over his third eye and send energy into it. Ask him to do something for you, like caressing your breasts, squeezing your bottom, kissing your neck. Use your upper energy center (throat, third eye, and crown) to connect with his. Talking and laughing helps.

Big Dick Syndrome: Does He Measure Up?

You may not care at all, but most men do care about size. Women know if it feels good, it is good. But somewhere along the way men got a ruler stuck into their heads. (And by the way, he might not understand why you're obsessed with your bottom, either.)

There's nothing you can do about actual size, but you can help relieve his anxiety by your own attitude of relaxed reassurance, sending him heart energy and diverting his attention. Stroking his ego won't hurt, either, by complimenting said member once in a while.

Challenges to Enchantresses

Going All the Way: Making Good Sex Even Better

Okay, everyone: You have imagination, orgasms, and enchanting skills. What else do you need? Communication. Know how to guide your lover to bring you to bliss.

Do this with "Ah," "Oh that feels so good," "Right there, yes, yes, yes." And so on. Groan, moan, or sigh, just use your vocal cords to add to the experience and subtly let him know how sexy it feels.

Whatever you do, no straight talk. It's not intimate or romantic to explain how Tab A should go into Slot B.

Can This Problem Be Licked?—No Magic Kiss for You

Whether it's because of a bad experience or inexperience, some men just don't go for "going down." You may desire a little more than you're getting, so you can try a few of these techniques to see if he'll do an about-face.

First, check yourself out, girl. If you're not "fresh," don't expect him to be eager to have you for dessert. We only mean "clean"—no air-freshening douches. Once you check out fine, move on to our techniques.

GETTING YOUR JUST DESERTS

Try the *9½ Weeks* method of reprogramming his aesthetic orientation. Set the scene and seduction for a sensual taste test. By that we mean blindfold him and feed him various foods (play with textures and tastes).

Remove the blindfold, then go down on him, but don't finish him. Ask him to do the same for you. Take cream, jam, honey, chocolate sauce—whatever he likes, and drizzle it down your torso, ending at your root.

Put your hand on his throat center and send blue light through it.

If he still doesn't want to try or doesn't like it, you're out of luck. You can lead a horse to water but you can't make him drink.

Whatever you do, do not hold intercourse hostage to get what you want, unless you want to risk your relationship. One has nothing to do with other, and love is not expressed by technique and demands.

Are You Coming?—The Absent Orgasm

Have you ever had one? If not, try masturbating. Start with the Breath of Passion or Root Stoking to get your root going, then put your hand down on your root center, massage and play with your body until you start an "itch" that needs to be scratched. You can use a sex video, a magazine, or erotic literature to get yourself going, and you can also get yourself a vibrator to help find your own pleasure.

The most frequent obstacle to orgasm is tension. Try to be relaxed, comfortable with yourself. Once you've done it on your own, it will be easier to do it with someone else.

Do not measure your sexual prowess or pleasure by your orgasms, the number or depth thereof. Sex is a connection and exchange with your consort, not a contest to climax.

Faking an orgasm can be an act of compassion (for your lover) and help you relax, but don't make that all you do. You'll be denying yourself a wonderful experience, and he'll never learn how to bring you to climax.

When you've figured out what you like, and feel comfortable, show him. He'll probably love it. And you can use any of the techniques and personas in this book to help you find a way to experiment.

THE BIG O EXERCISE

On a Friday and prior to making love, light a red candle, breathe the color red into your root and navel centers. Dab musk on your root. While you're with your lover, concentrate on the sensual connection between you. Try to feel the give and take. Allow your excitement to mount and keep feeding your root. Don't strive for an orgasm, just stay with the sensation. Try to lose yourself in the feeling.

It's No Choke: Oral Sex

This is one time when men love to receive but women don't often love to give. See "The Kiss of Magic" in Chapter Two for an approach that may make this easier for you.

If you get all choked up just thinking about it, try to improve your gag reflex. Take a lollipop and press down on the back of your tongue. Then slowly move it forward. Practice moving it back and forth slowly.

When you do it with him, only use your tongue until you feel ready for more. You don't have to know exactly how to perform perfect oral sex. Your consort can tell you what he likes and no doubt he'll enjoy instructing you. There's no way to go wrong with this one, but please, no teeth.

What's Your Hurry?—Prolonging Sex

If you're in the heat of passion and you want it to go on, don't stop completely and take a breather. Instead, pull your

WEB energy toward you. You can slow the pulse connection, which will slow the pace. Also, during intercourse, pull your root energy up into your pelvis. This is hard to do at first, so practice with it when you feel relaxed about your results.

The Second Coming: Raising It Up Again

When his pecker's popped and you still want some action, try this, but don't begin too quickly. He needs some space and time to juice up and recharge. You risk putting the fire out if you fan it too forcefully.

Send him root energy from your own root, in an even flow. Since the experience of lovemaking stays in your body longer, you'll find it easier to restart and fuel him.

With the slow rhythm of postsex, wrap him in your WEB. Also, through your brow center, send him erotic suggestions. Draw him toward you with some playful gesture (kissing on the neck) and allow him to respond. If your passion doesn't reignite, just cuddle. Don't feel as if you failed, because he'll sense it and a new problem will arise.

Oh No!—The Aborted Orgasm

Some women feel themselves coming very quickly but instead hold back to wait for their consort's orgasm. Doing this can inhibit your orgasm altogether. If you feel as if you missed your orgasm and can't get back to it, you need to reconnect with your root. Let your energy undulate down to your root from your upper body, and use his rhythm to rekindle your flame.

Let's Make a Deal: Getting What You Want

When you're aching for a particular pleasure which your consort is not inclined to provide, you can play "Let's Make a Deal." By this we mean trading favors—scratch his back and he'll scratch yours. This tactic is playfully transactional, but it does communicate how much you want your desire fulfilled. Then maybe he'll become spontaneously generous. (You never know!)

Body Image and Other Holy Grails

Body Image is one of the tyrannies of our times. Everyone is supposed to be twenty years old, with a perfect body (whatever that is this month). It is like the Holy Grail, an impossible perfection, and there are women throwing up or starving themselves trying to achieve it. Even the beautiful women in the magazines today won't be there tomorrow. So if you happen to fit the current ideal, you are not going to keep it.

Those who do keep their beauty are the ones who appreciate themselves. If you are in touch your sexuality and are confident of your "self," you emit a glow that is attractive at any age. You may not be conventionally beautiful, you may not be the first person someone sees in a room, but you are attractive.

A lot of body image problems stem from fear of rejection. We know there are hurtful things that can happen if you don't fall within certain physical parameters. You can be insulted for being overweight, overtly sexy, too skinny, whatever. We've all felt this at some point. Know that you're not alone. While there are people whose looks are held up as ideal, this has nothing to do with you and your attractiveness. A person who feels attractive, *is* attractive. And that's that. Find your self-acceptance and you're on your way.

See the first chapter to find how to express your inner self and bring your inner beauty to the surface. Truly looking in the mirror and not to others for your reflection will help give you back your sense of self.

If you need a boost for your self-esteem and love worthiness, try this exercise. It is best done when the moon is waxing.

CONJURING ATTRACTIVENESS

Dress in something that makes you feel beautiful and sensual. By candlelight, anoint your heart center with lavender. Open your root center and your brow center. Feel their energies. Look into a mirror.

Say aloud:

Aphrodite's passion flow
Share with me all that you know.
Beauty, lust, and sexy wiles,
I have the charm to allure and beguile.
I claim my power on this night
And know it is my womanly right.
So be it.
And so it is.

If you're not in the mood, hold off and wait until you are. Then repeat as necessary.

Yo! Girlfriend! A Word on Attitude

Remember, everyone gets rejected—even the people you most admire. So watch how you deal with your own rejection.

Try not to crumble or get too upset about it. If you collapse from rejection, you are handing your power over to the very putz who didn't appreciate it. This will diminish your allure. On the other hand, if you get really enraged, your anger can turn into a shield that prevents anyone else from approaching you.

It is natural to feel anger or sadness, so do let it out, just don't get stuck in it. Feel it, then try to move on. Don't be afraid to let go—it doesn't mean your relationship or affection was meaningless.

If you need further help to boost you back into bewitching splendor, check out the Resurrecting the Goddess exercise in Chapter 8.

Releasing Inhibitions

Most inhibitions come from shame. First, know the difference between what you don't like and what you're actually inhibited about. For instance, if you don't like to be on top during sex because you don't like the way your stomach looks, that is about shame; whereas not wanting to slide into the lime green Jell-O bath with him is just a preference.

The best way to start is to visualize yourself doing whatever it is that inhibits you. Watch how you act in your fantasy and learn from it. Then, all you have to do (gulp) is talk to your consort about trying it.

It's always helpful to preface your conversation by saying it is difficult for you to talk about. This will predispose him to listen compassionately. You might also try a little lavender on your heart center so you don't feel so nervous.

FEAR RELEASE

On a Monday during a waning moon, light a white candle, place an ice cube(s) in a bowl. Surround yourself with white light.

Say aloud:

As the ice melts so do my inhibitions and shame.

I affirm I am safe and protected as I melt the barriers to self-acceptance and experimentation. I release my fear and the judgments of others that have negatively affected my life.

Repeat as needed. This is a useful ritual for releasing other fears as well; just change the words.

No/Low Libido

Sometimes you feel like a nut, sometimes you don't. There's nothing wrong with it. All relationships go through hot and cool periods.

Nurturing, closeness, and intimacy are all keys to rekindling sexual desire. Taken in little increments, they can help fuel a spark into a flame. Read on to see if there is ongoing affection in your relationship and use the bewitching enchantments.

FUELING THE FLAME

During a waxing moon, pick a Tuesday night when you are sure your consort will be home for dinner. Before he arrives, light a large red candle and sit before it. Gaze at the candle, breathing the heat from the flame into your heart and pulling it down to your root. Feel a warm glow building there. Place your hands over your root if it helps you, or hold the candle in front of it. When you are ready, place your hands on the floor and aloud, call on the Goddess Artemis to ask for her help in feeling your fire. (Artemis is the Goddess of untamed abandonment.)

If you are now in the mood, leave the candle burning and when your lover comes home, share cheese and fruit from a single plate, and drink wine or cider from the same glass. Snuggle in and see what happens.

Note: Libido is also adversely affected by depression, physical ailments, a hypothyroid condition, and some antidepressants. If you're experiencing a prolonged period of disinterest or you have a sneaking suspicion that there's something wrong, digging deeper may be necessary to find the true source of the problem.

Beyond Bewitchery

If your enchantments haven fallen flat of late, the source of your difficulties may not be sex but may lie elsewhere in your life. Sex is often used as a scapegoat when it is only a secondary symptom of another issue.

A breakdown in your physical intimacy usually has its origins in your emotional life and/or a collapse of communication.

Use this checklist to see if any of these situations sound familiar.

Situations Beyond Sorcery

For him

- Is he overworked?
- Is he worried about money?
- Has he been rejected or passed over at work?
- Is he experiencing a life crisis?
- Is he depressed?
- Is he bothered by signs of aging?
- Is he drinking too much or smoking marijuana or doing other drugs?

You can try talking to him about any of these problems, but many men won't respond. Do not take this personally; it is the way most men react. However, ask compassionate questions, just let him know that you're there, and reassure him that the problems will pass. But don't let the situation go on too long without suggesting therapy or couples therapy.

If neither of you confronts your problems, you could risk having your relationship break up. Denial never works for long. Men who won't work on their issues often look to rekindle themselves through a spark of passion—which means they turn to someone new. Women tend to turn on themselves, suffer low self-esteem, and get depressed.

For you

- Are you using sex to prove you are still attractive?
- Are you harboring feelings of resentment or anger?

- Are you getting your period?
- Are you staying in a relationship that is really over?
- Have you been giving too much?
- Are you very tired?
- Have you taken time to be alone with him? by yourself?
- Do you have natural downtime to "allow" sex to happen.
- Are you drinking, smoking marijuana, or doing other drugs more than usual?
- Are you depressed?

If you answered yes to any of the above, try to alleviate the problem at its source. You can talk to your consort about it, consult a therapist or a friend, go to couples therapy. Sex isn't the issue here.

Okay? Read on for more magic.

THE HUSBAND WHO SAW HIS WIFE WITH ANOTHER MAN

A peasant lay in wait inside
His house to see what could be spied.
He saw another man instead
Of him, enjoying his wife in bed.
"Alas," he said, "what have I seen?"
His wife replied: "What do you mean?
Fair lord, my love, what did you see?"
"Another man, I'm sure," said he,
"Was on the bed in your embrace."
His wife, with anger in her face,
Replied, "A man? Oh, very well,
You're sick again, that I can tell.
You cling to lies, as if they're true."
"I trust my eyes—that I must do."
"You're mad," she said, "to think you can
Insist you saw me with a man.
Now tell the truth, at once, be good."
"I saw him leaving for the wood."
"Oh no!" she said, "that means that I
Today or next day'll surely die.
It happened to my Gran, you see,
My mother, too, and now to me.
It happened just before they died—
A fact well-known both far and wide,
A young man led both off, you know—
They had no other cause to go.
My end is near, the die is cast—

Send for my cousins, I need them fast.
Let's split up all our property—
I mustn't waste my time, you see.
With all the stuff that is my share,
I'll to a nunnery repair."
The peasant heard, and cried in fear:
"Let be, let be, my sweetheart, dear,
Don't leave me now, like this, I pray—
I made up all I saw today."
"I dare not stay, it's far too late—
I'm thinking of my spiritual state,
Especially, after the shame
That you've attached to my good name.
I will be blamed, I know I will
For treating you so very ill,
Unless, perhaps, you'd rather swear,
With all my family standing there,
You never saw a man with me.
You must swear also, don't you see?
This subject will be dropped and you
Will never nag me for it, too."
He answered "Lady, I agree."
They both went off to church, and he
Soon swore to all she'd asked him for
All that, ah yes, and much much more.

—MARIE OF FRANCE

SEVEN

General Sorcery for Relationship Troubleshooting

Yes, sexual bewitchery goes beyond the bedroom and can be used in your relationship. Don't forget—problems are not all his or yours. You participate in them mutually.

In this very useful chapter, you will learn some great ways to shift the energy (and take the pressure off) such mating maladies as:

Jealousy
Obsession
Manipulators and controllers
Anger
Separation

Releasing the past
Infidelity
Yearning

If you want to self-diagnose, read along. Don't be surprised to find that there's a little of each in every relationship. Focus on the one(s) that seem to be the most problematic for you and your consort.

Jealousy: The Not-So-Jolly Green Giant

Even in the most confident and charmed relationships, there's a certain amount of jealousy. It's natural but it becomes an issue when it happens too often, or the shadow of the Green Giant looms between you.

Jealousy can stem from

- Insecurity
- Possessiveness
- Problems with change or risk
- Fear of rejection or separation
- Feelings of inadequacy

Jealousy rests in the root and third centers; it is essentially a power struggle with sexual overtones.

The Psychic Destruction of Jealousy

Jealousy can be a self-fulfilling prophecy. It breeds a distrust that destroys relationships. It is also a denial of love—with the jealous person not trusting or accepting the love he or she is given. This resistance makes him constantly suspicious of his lover. Over time, the heart connection will fray and break, thus creating the reality she fears most.

Should you always give in to your consort in order to keep the peace? No. Kowtowing to the demands of a jealous person can also dim your light. Being admired gives you an energy that you take back to your relationship. If you're denied this, there are two reactions. One, you can become a shadow of yourself and lose your identity other than being your consort's appendage. Two, all that pent-up energy of yours explodes, often breaking up the relationship. Neither of these options is very attractive or constructive.

How to Heal the Green Blues

These exercises are the same for either the possessee or possessor. Scents that open space are very good (vanilla and lavender). Decorate your home with natural objects and things that bring in a sense of lightness—bows of pine, flowers, feathers, amethysts. Since jealous energy is very tight, these will all help to relax the jealous person and help the mate to cope. Clearing is also very important.

An all-important tip: When jealousy hits, don't forget to breathe! This can make all the difference.

DEFLATING YOUR GREEN GIANT

This is an ongoing antidote for your jealousy. Keep clearing your third center with either salt or smudge; start to be conscious of what tightens it up. It is a signal that you are heading into trouble. Breathe space into your WEB when you feel either jealousy or constriction, either from him or you, and don't wear the color yellow. Surround your consort in pink light to open up the connection you share.

There isn't much you can do about the power center problem if it belongs to your consort. All you can do is keep the heart connection open and set your limits—how much are you going to modify your behavior to accommodate his needs? Know your limits and do not allow yourself to be stifled. If you continue, it will be difficult to feel radiant, and it will spill over into creativity and life in general. It is too high a price to pay.

To sum up, the consequences of unchecked jealousy are very unpleasant.

Obsession

> "Compulsive preoccupation with a fixed idea or an unwanted feeling or emotion, often accompanied by symptoms of anxiety."
>
> —*American Heritage Dictionary*

Our friend, Allison, is a prime example of obsessive behavior.

She came over for lunch one day. Here's a sample of her conversation, which went on nonstop for thirty-five minutes.

ALLISON: So I told you that Roy has this big meeting on Monday, right? I mean it's really a big deal, it could mean a new account for him, he might even get a car in it. . . .

US: Yes, you told us when you came in.

ALLISON: And so he went to look for a new tie last night to

go with his navy pinstripe—don't you think that's a good thing to wear to a meeting?—anyway, and I told him I'd help him choose his tie even though I had scheduled dinner with Julie, my friend who just had an operation . . .

US: You mean you canceled dinner with your friend who just got out of the hospital?!

ALLISON: . . . but he told me not to bother to go with him and that I should see Julie. So Julie and I just happened to have dinner at a restaurant near his favorite store.

US: Uh-huh. Sure.

ALLISON: So we just walked in and I bought him a tie (just in case he didn't find one), and he wasn't there. I mean, we were there for at least an hour . . .

US: Poor Julie . . .

ALLISON: . . . Do you think he really went to that store or do you think I should worry that maybe he had a secret date? I mean he has been acting a little strange lately. I guess I would be able to find out through his credit card receipts, but then he might have paid cash . . .

We looked at each other, looked at her, and said, "It's time for a chat."

Allison was not in the mood to listen, but then we brought up the perils of obsession: **If you don't get a hold of yourself, your obsession will drive him away.**

That got her attention.

Check yourself with our list—if you are inclined to behave this way when you're well into the relationship, you are in the possession of obsession.

- Do you constantly put him first?
- Do you disregard your own needs?

- Do you always build your plans around him?
- Do you connect every little errand you do to him?
- Do you feel as if your life would be over if he left you?
- Do you feel obligated to solve his problems or help him in every possible way?
- Do you constantly ask your friends for advice and not take it?

(This behavior is perfectly normal in the first months of falling in love, but then you *both* feel it.)

If you've answered "yes" to any of these, you are possessed by the Demon Obsession.

Exorcisms for Obsession

12 Practical Steps for Depossession

1. Recognize that you are obsessed.
2. Affirm that you want to release the obsession (this is the hardest part). Give up the belief that you have to hold on so hard to keep him.
3. Keep track of how often you think about him or talk about him. Set a limit and stick to it.
4. Notice how often you build your plans around him or make decisions based on what he likes. Consider what you'd like to do if you weren't worried about him. Then do it.
5. Stop talking to your friends about him—just listen to them.
6. When he asks you to do something, don't always do it just because he wants you to.

7. Never change your schedule for him unless it is for a really, really good reason.
8. Go away for a weekend without him.
9. Start asking him to do things for you.
10. Start making time for your friends and other activities.
11. Get out there and flirt.
12. Plan your life so that it goes on with or without him.

Behind the Scenes of Obsession: A Psychic Power Outage

Obsession is a seriously damaging psychic practice. You are freely giving your power to someone who hasn't asked for it. Your attempts to generate a one-way energetic chain in order to keep your consort attached to you are not natural and are damned uncomfortable for both of you.

The longer this goes on, the more your power drains from you and the more he becomes crucial (in your mind only!) to your continued existence. This, as you might imagine, is a recipe for disaster.

You cannot be a powerful enchantress under these conditions. It's time to cast this demon out.

THE EXORCISM: PART I

This is to be conducted on a full moon (even if you have a date with him).

Take a shower with sea salt and make sure you rub it on each of your seven sources, back and front.

Sit quietly with your feet on the ground.

Light a white candle.

Place a knife in front of you.

Anoint both the front and back of your body along the seven centers with lavender scented oil or water. Start at the root and work up.

Breathe the appropriate color through each center, opening them as much as possible. (You might find it hard to open the second center.)

Pick up the knife.

Slice through the air around yourself.

Say aloud:

I call on Hecate the Wise One to help me slay the demon obsession.

I cut the negative connections between me and (his name) with the sword of compassion.

I allow myself to be guided in this process, knowing that I am safe and nurtured by the Goddess herself.

I affirm the space is open for this healing, both within my heart and in my life.

I turn this over to the greater good with faith that this will be done.

So be it. And so it is.

Repeat as often as necessary until the new moon.

OBSESSION: PART II

Reclaiming your power.

On the new moon, shower again with sea salt.

Light a red and a yellow candle.

Anoint your root at the front (on the pubic bone) and the back (at the base of your spine) with a dab of peppermint oil. Do the same with your solar plexus, front and back.

Sit before the flames, gaze at them, breathe in their fire.

Pick up the red candle. Hold it before your root center. Breathe in its light and warmth.

Say aloud:

> With this candle I reclaim my life force, my will, my belief in my ability to live with or without a partner. I direct my root to the earth, its source.

Set down the red candle and pick up the yellow one.

Hold it before your solar plexus.

Say aloud:

> I use this flame to reignite my own power, my own force, to express my individuality in the world, with or without a partner.

Feel your centers expand with the energy and say aloud:

> I affirm my place in the world.
> So be it. And so it is.

Manipulators and Controllers

First things first: Who's doing the manipulating and who's receiving it? Are you dangling your consort from strings or are you the one running around? And don't tell us you've never met a man like this. We could each name ten right off the bat. If you really can't think of anyone, try taking a look in the mirror. Who have you been browbeating?

Everyone has a little manipulation or control inside; it's part of human nature. However, it becomes a problem if one of you is consistently dominating the other (unless you gave him the whip last Christmas and you love spending time on your knees).

If you're not sure whether your situation warrants attention, see how familiar these control situations sound.

- He often comments on how you look and offers to help you look the way he prefers.
- He tells you what to wear when you're meeting his friends or family (without your request for advice).
- He orders for you in restaurants.
- He tells you to lose or gain weight.
- He insists you live by his schedule.
- He constantly criticizes the way you do things.
- He makes big decisions without asking your opinion.
- He accuses you of sneaking around behind his back.
- The more assertive and independent you get, the more he wants to hang on to you.
- He has people checking up on you.
- He has total control over your finances.
- He decides what problems to share with you.

If you can substitute "I" for "he," it's you who needs to get out of the driver's seat.

Manipulators are not so obvious. They'll have you thinking that you're the controlling one: Their tool is guilt. Manipulation is *not,* as some people think, asking a straight question and expecting yes for an answer. It's when a request is couched is such a way it isn't a request at all.

For instance, your lover wants to go to the Caribbean,

knowing full well you've been looking forward to skiing. Does he say

1. I'd really love it if we went south this winter?
2. Look at this picture of Aruba. You know, you have been looking a little peaked lately. The sun is just what you need. Even your mother thinks it would do you a world of good. Why don't we go?

The manipulator gets his way by persuading you it is what you want. Whether it is or not.

Passive-aggressive types are even more infuriating; they won't act, leaving you to take all the action, then they'll have the final say-so. (ARGH!!!)

Chances are, you've run into one or more of the above. Here's what you do: Call him on it and work it out with him or say good-bye. We mean it; you have to be willing to let him go or it's not going to work.

You're engaging in a third center power play rather than an affair of the root or the heart. Your psychic energy is tainted by this struggle so you need to clear it out before you act.

PUSHING THE POWER BUTTON: CLEARING THE CONTROL

On any day during the waning moon, light a yellow candle and place a bowl of sea salt in front of it.

Have a smudge stick and a glass of water at hand.

Brush your hand over/through the flame (you won't get burned if you are quick).

Rub your hands in the salt.

Light the smudge stick and clear your third center with the smoke (and anywhere else you like)

Drink the water.

Say aloud:

With the flame I purge this tie
And his control I now deny.
With the salt this earth will heal
to let me know if his love is real.
Smoke and air will carry 'way
the negative thoughts I think today.
And through my body this water can clear
the way to see the truth, not fear.

Hold your solar plexus with both hands. Breathe into it and exhale sharply. See how you feel—fearful? relaxed? reborn? hopeful?

You may find that this exercise evokes nausea. This is the recalibration of your power center. Allow yourself to settle out for a few days.

Once you've cleared, you're ready to take back your power and confront your consort.

Confronting Your Consort

Prepare a list of examples and the points you want to make and write them down ahead of time. This serves two purposes. First, you'll remember why you're doing this, and second, he won't be able to take over by using his usual methods to bamboozle you if you are well-equipped. Write your list in a neutral environment or your own place. His psychic energy is too strong on his own turf.

PART I: COURAGE BOOSTER

On a Tuesday during a waxing moon, light a bright yellow candle. Gather any power objects that give you a positive sense of yourself, such as your business card, keepsakes from loved ones, shells or stones you've collected, medals or certificates you've won. Have at least four and place them around you. Sit before the candle and breathe in the energy of the flame (not the flame itself).

Close your eyes and see yourself speaking clearly and compassionately from your list. See your consort listening and respecting you. Know that you are heard.

PART II: THE POWER POWWOW

Choose a Friday when you are together with plenty of time and no distractions. Insist on it. When you are comfortable, tell him that you have serious concerns about your relationship and that he has to listen or things will be beyond repair.

Wear yellow and/or silk and/or an agate medallion (jasper and marble are okay, too) over your solar plexus. (We've tied it to our bras.)

Surround yourself with white light and go for it. Spare him nothing, but speak from your heart. Try to stay away from accusations, since you have cooperated with him up to now and he is probably not aware of what he's been doing to hurt you. This could very well be a surprise to him.

There's likely to be a scene. No one likes to be told he is wrong, and no one likes to give up control.

Let things settle for a few days, to see if he has any intention of changing. Then you can begin the slow road to reconnection or disconnection. Make your own decision from here. (If he remains entrenched, we encourage you to see Bewitching Breakups, in this chapter.)

If the control in your relationship has escalated to the point where he is emotionally or physically abusive, don't bother to talk it out. He either needs to get help or you need to leave. It's beyond magical repair.

If You're at the Controls

If you're the controller, you need to understand the roots of your behavior. It's next to impossible to do this on your own (after all, you can't be objective about yourself). If you're really brave, you can ask your lover (if he sticks around) to point it out.

One clue to look for: If your consort asks you to sit down with him and he has a list of examples, you're in trouble.

Hot Heads, Cold Hearts: How to Deal with His Anger and Yours

Do you express your anger in a healthy way? Here's how to find out.

Anger Quiz

1. You're picking up underwear from the bedroom floor for the forty-first time. He steps over you to pick up his briefcase. You:

- ***a.*** Bite his ankle.
- ***b.*** Say "Excuse me" and get out of his way.
- ***c.*** Throw his underwear in his face and say, "Hey, you forgot this and by the way, you owe me $120 for cleaning services for the last two weeks."

2. You see him kissing a voluptuous redhead at a cocktail party. You:

- ***a.*** Dump your drink on the redhead and slap him silly.
- ***b.*** Say nothing but go and cry in the bathroom.
- ***c.*** Confront him after he disengages and leave with or without him.

3. You're driving him to the station in your car. He constantly comments on the way you drive while slamming his foot on an imaginary brake. You:

- ***a.*** Fake veering into a tree in order to shut him up.
- ***b.*** Struggle to obey his directions, muttering, "I'm sorry."
- ***c.*** Pull over and tell him he can walk if he can't ride like a gentleman.

If you've answered *a* to most of the questions you have serial killer anger and might benefit from kickboxing instead of kicking your partner; *b* answers indicate you're on the road to martyrdom and don't think that you're not angry—you're just afraid of confrontation; and *c* means you know what anger feels like and you share it with him very constructively.

Anger is natural to every relationship and it doesn't pay to avoid it; you'll just end up with more problems. Anger is part of passion, a natural clearing process, for both the root and the solar plexus centers.

To help you deal with your anger, add a little heart energy to your communication (when possible) so that you don't annihilate your partner.

After you've exploded or otherwise released your anger, breathe deeply, loosen your energy, then feel your feet firmly on the ground. Bring some passion down into your root and into your heart and keep breathing. You might get rigid during and after an angry tirade, which can make you unapproachable. Easing off your anger does not make you weak or indicate surrender.

> Visualize clearing the third center, both yours and his. Speak from your heart. Do not immediately touch him, but start connecting your heart chakra to his.

This gives him the space to take in your anger, digest it, and respond—if he is ready. *You* need to stay open to his response.

He gets angry too. When he's the one exploding, try to remember, he's just clearing his centers and don't take it personally. Don't make his anger a part of your feelings. You can protect yourself when he blows his stack by covering your solar plexus with your arms and sending him energy through your heart center. Keep breathing—and this will both help protect you from his lava flow and calm him down.

When All the Fuses Blow

When you're both screaming, it's hard to do any sort of bewitchery. Your connections are overloaded and it might be hard to find your heart (and his) again.

Here's what you do.

First, figure out what it is that makes you so angry (and look below the surface—it may not be how often you clean the house, but generally feeling that you're taken for granted). If you don't know what you're mad about, try meditating on it. (See Appendix B: Meditation Practices.)

Within a day or two, come back to the topic to see if it has cleared. First connect your centers with his, then speak from the heart.

If your explosions of anger have become a regular event, talk to him when things are calm. You can always do the rejoining exercises if you feel your connection has weakened.

Some of us use anger to create passion. It's great to make up after a fight, and sex is usually very lusty. But this can be an addictive pattern that will eventually come apart. Clearly you need more than anger to sustain a good relationship.

Note: Chronic anger can also signal depression.

How Can I Live Without You? Separation Anxiety

Separations come in many varieties. Some nice, some not. They can range from an overnight business trip to a trial parting before deciding to divorce.

Being parted from your lover, regardless of the length of time, means you are living within a different psychic energy than when you lived together. When you are in contact with the same person day in and day out, you start to weave together. With your partner out of the picture, you may feel oddly incomplete.

Many of us see separation as threatening to the security of our relationship. Lack of trust makes the separation and coming together again even harder. We've even seen couples fight before or after a separation, expressing their resentment at being left and providing a natural opportunity to kiss and make up. This method is not terribly skillful and wastes a lot of time getting to the good stuff.

To ease the sting of separation, it is good to have a talisman or keepsake from your lover. Have a jeweler cut a crystal in half, or simply exchange personal objects (not your wedding rings) like one of a pair of earrings or cufflinks.

If you want to make a deeper impression, use scent. You will find that a piece of clothing that he's worn is very evocative and warming, while your own fragrance on one of your silk scarves will provide him with an equally powerful reminder.

You can send your absent partner heart energy—but if you're feeling desperate, clear yourself first and breathe deeply. (To expand your aura see WEB Wrap, Chapter 4.) When you're ready, send him a thought from your heart center while you are holding whatever you have of his. Send a message to him through your brow center such as, "I would like to hear from you tonight," but do it without feeling like it must happen. This is not a test.

Root energy is best sent when you have the person on the phone. The power of your voice and the pulse of your root will hook his sexual connection to you. If you send him root energy randomly, you could be increasing his libido while he's in someone else's company, not the best idea unless you're trying to get rid of him.

Just a quick note on the upside of separation. Nothing stimulates a relationship more than bringing new things into it. Furthermore, it gives you a chance to discover yourself. Separations in good relationships strengthen and rekindle connections. So send him off with a cheerful smile, a scented scarf, and a few preset phone dates.

Then settle back and enjoy your space.

Welcome Home Bewitchery

Hilda's Homecoming for Harry

Hilda's long-term live-in lover, Harry, was returning from a month-long business trip. Hilda was used to Harry's absences for three or four days, but this trip had seemed overly long. Although they had exchanged a few phone calls, Hilda felt as if she were going on her first date as she prepared to go to the airport to pick him up. She raised her goddess energy and wove her WEB with anticipation.

Harry arrived and gave her an awkward peck while they walked toward the exit. Hilda noticed his brusque demeanor but remembered that this was typical of Harry's shy behavior. She followed him until he realized he didn't know where the car was and turned to her in amusement. They laughed and he hugged her.

When they got home, she suggested he shower since Harry was determined to beat his jet lag and stay up until the sun went down.

Next, Hilda shuttled Harry out of doors for a walk in nature to use the elements for their reconnection.

They walked down to the riverfront near their house,

and Hilda remarked how nice it was to be outside. They sat by the river's edge and enjoyed its flow, feeling the breeze on their faces as the sun set.

Harry started playing with her hair and suggested they return home. Hilda repeated her natural elements theme at home with candles, flowers, champagne, grapes, and smoked salmon sandwiches. They raised their glasses and toasted each other. After a few nibbles they retired into the bedroom. Hilda left the curtain open to reveal the night sky, and they made love, consciously weaving their energies back together. All's well that ends well.

Returning and Reconnecting

You too can create a smooth and easy reconnection after a separation. Just go back to WEB weaving and use the elements to help you rejoin your rhythms.

Remember, you're both different from being apart and it isn't bad. Preferably in a quiet moment, breathe and send your energy into his, starting from the root. Gently connect your centers. Don't pull too hard—keep it soft and flowing. You will be much more successful if you keep your heart open. You can share the process with him, both consciously breathing into each center in turn. It doesn't have to be long or elaborate.

Try heart holding, too. Place his hand over your heart center and yours over his. Just breathe and be together in silence. Not all men are comfortable with these practices, so you can always take Hilda's example and just quietly enact reconnection by yourself.

Here are some suggestions for both of you to do together to reconnect through the elements.

Fire

Sit by candlelight
Watch the sun set
Sit in front of the fireplace
Barbecue

Earth

Take a walk in nature
Plant something
Eat something
Exchange tokens

Air

Say "I love you"
Burn incense
Star gaze
Ask him questions/engage in conversation

Water

Take a bath or shower together
Drink something
Walk along a body of water
Water your garden

The Sexual Doldrums

Once you realize you're in the sexual doldrums, you're going to get scared. Is there something wrong in your relationship? Chances are not—it's most likely just a phase.

Resist the impulse to clutch him to you. If you try to pull him in, your need may make him feel suffocated or anxious; you could turn a simple ebb in passion into a veritable pressure cooker.

Remember, men go through cycles also. Your relationship is not just about you. It is a dance between attraction and space—this is what creates interest. Use your bewitching skills to find his readiness switch. All the seductive suggestions in Chapter 3 are an excellent resource. Then concentrate on the root and the heart when you send the energy into him. Bring the feminine into your house: candlelight, flowers, etc. Think of yourself as the Empress archetype, nurturing and holding, regal and powerful.

Reigniting Interest

Mystery is the mistress of a good relationship. To stir up his interest and ignite your own, try some of these tips.

- Leave him alone from time to time—don't be around constantly. Make plans with friends. Give him time on his own.
- Show yourself in the best light. Make sure that he doesn't see you in your old underwear or dirty sweats.
- Look for opportunities to "vogue." Wrap a towel around you so it drapes down to the small of your back—most women look good this way. Use your hair as a seductive tool by letting it fall in front of your eyes to peer through.
- Constantly give him fleeting, tantalizing glimpses of your attractiveness. Try high heels, corsets, stockings, even (or most especially) when you're not doing anything special.
- Concentrate on other things. Be genuinely absorbed in

something else, but be in the same room as him. Put pedicured, bare feet up on your couch while you read.

If you're too stuck in the "blahs" to be bothered with these little enticements, it may be because you feel unattractive or out of touch with your feminine source. If this is the case, go back to Chapter 6 and do the exercise for gathering your self-esteem (see Body Image and the Holy Grail).

Severing Connections with Past Lovers

Joining sexually with someone creates an energetic connection that lasts, whether or not the person remains in your life. From a one-night stand to a long-term relationship, this person has some link to you. So having many lovers can build up a big old pile of baggage.

There are other facts, too. If you're constantly with a lot of men and find that sex has become mechanical, you could be trying to fill a need for love or approval with sex. Try to be discerning about whom you honor with your enchanting skills.

So now that you know what you're carrying around with you, you may want to clear it away.

EXERCISE TO CLEAR PAST SEXUAL CONNECTIONS

Repeat this exercise over several days while the moon is waning. (You don't have to be exact about whom you're clearing.)

Monday for the hidden connections.
Friday for love connections.
Saturday for releasing any remaining blockages.

1. Light a white candle, place a bowl of water in front of you. Concentrate on your root center and then on any other center that feels right, the third and fourth come up most often.

2. Take a white spool of thread. Hold it in front of each center you feel needs clearing (definitely do your root). Pull thread out from the spool and break it off.

3. Say aloud:
I release connections that no longer serve me. (If you wish, you can elaborate with specific situations and/or people.)

4. When you are finished, burn the threads.

5. Clear yourself and the room with smudge. Breathe into each center to realign yourself.

Psychic side effects: As part of the healing process, that person (or someone like him) may resurrect himself in your life. His reappearance may make you feel sad, but understand this is all part of the healing process. (This exercise can unstick current relationships and/or make you feel free and more open to a new one.)

The Bewitching Breakup

Before you break up with someone, do the clearing of past connections exercise skipping step four. Keep the pieces of thread by the candle until after you have broken up with the person. Then, on a Saturday night, light the candle, repeat the words, burn the threads, and clear your centers.

Infidelity—Cavorting consorts

May we be the first to say that there is far too much hysteria around infidelity in our culture, partially because there is too much emphasis on coupledom and partially because what is a natural human expression is looked upon as an unnatural act.

While we are told that human beings do not mate for life, as exemplified by our divorce rate, we're also told we must. Being faithful is having a heartfelt partnership, not solely an exclusive physical commitment, although that can accompany it.

As much as you may not want to admit it, men behave differently from women. Men have a constantly active radar screen that blips whenever an attractive female approaches. It doesn't matter if they're married to the spitting image of Nicole Kidman, they love to look and, frankly, we love being admired. Women usually just enjoy the "looking" phase. Men are prone to go further.

Even if you are in the happiest of unions, you may be faced with some form of infidelity. Don't panic. You aren't alone, and there are many different ways to deal with it.

1. Lapses, Ooopseys, and Other Dalliances

If you happen to find that your consort has been cavorting, take a deep breath before you react. There is a chance that this was a short-term oopsey and no more than that—a flash in the pan, a one-night wonder, a quickie. Men are curious. Sometimes they have a *head* for trouble.

Momentary lapses like a one-nighter on a business trip or some brief entanglement happen. Of course, you're hurt. You can get mad, maybe even break a few dishes (not over his head please). But then settle down and realize what this can bring you.

If you forgive him, and you will if you are a wise woman, it can improve your relationship. He will be very grateful for your understanding (and you have our permission to milk it for a bit if you want). You may also find that your sex life improves—your passion and your interest level heighten. Your commitment has taken a blow and survived.

However, even in a brief lapse, your trust will be shaken. You may find it takes a while to build it back. This is natural. Go with your instincts, keeping in mind that relationship snags can actually benefit your relationship by opening communication and feelings.

2. Affairs (The Big Nasty)

An affair by our definition is a long-term (over three months) relationship with someone who isn't you. It is a warning sign that there is something amiss in your lives together. This is definitely not something to take lightly.

An affair can be a way to heal your relationship or to end it. It stirs up so much that you have to face your problems. The worse thing you can do is nothing. Problems may sink below the surface, but they don't go away.

If his affair devastates you, examine how much time and energy you have invested in being a "couple." Do you have an identity outside your relationship as an individual? If you don't, develop one. To get yourself going, see Chapters 1 through 3 and watch for reactions from other people (including him).

While it is natural to want to blame someone else, try not to concentrate on the "other woman." You don't want to do hard time for homicide, and she's not the problem.

Okay, so what can you do?

Rage, scream, rant, and show him what he means to you, how hurt you are. Be a crazy, raving siren. Avoid the weeping martyr, clutching, please-don't-leave-me gal. You'll feel better and you'll probably scare the bejesus out of him. Just don't do it in front of the kids.

Once the fireworks are over, sit down together and talk. Remember, his having an affair does not mean he does not love you. Here are some topics of conversation.

1. If you must, ask the basics (who, when, how) and be aware that this is the stuff of torture—yours not his. Knowing sometimes helps as your imagination will make it much better than it really was, but it will rub salt in the wound.
2. How does he feel about your relationship? (And if he says, "Not much, I'm outta here," he's just saved you a lot of trouble; happily show him the door.) If he says "she" makes him feel special, young, important, etc., realize that his problem may be rooted in his lack of self-esteem.
3. What is your part in this? No doubt you're listening to what he is saying and wondering where you went wrong. If you can figure it out, great. We suggest you go to a professional if you really want to work on your relationship. If you don't do it this time, there's a possibility that you'll find yourself in this position again.

We recommend you get help in any case, whether you stay together or not. Even if the relationship doesn't work out, you're likely to learn a lot and hopefully not repeat the past.

If the affair continues while you are still together, continue the clearing rituals. Reconnecting can also be ongoing during the infidelity stage.

The same applies if it is you who has strayed. You need to decide when and how you're going to deal with it in your relationship.

After the Storm

If the affair has ended for you and for him, and you decide to stay together, do a rejoining or a recommitment ritual.

RECONNECTING

1. On a Friday, during a waxing moon.
2. Clear together by taking a sea salt shower.
3. Sit opposite each other on the floor, naked or clothed.
4. Connect each energy center.
5. Hold each other's hands and look into each other's eyes.
6. Aloud, take turns saying what you feel about each other and affirm that you want to recommit.

7. Share a drink, some food, and relax together afterward in a cozy setting.

Yearning, an Unpleasant Side Effect of Love and Sex

Yearning is a natural feeling that can even be deliciously painful. Yearning is common to youth; it starts with your first crush on a rock star. For adults, it happens when your consort is away or when there is no one in your life.

When it can't be satisfied, yearning can get out of hand. It's very seductive, because of its bittersweet feeling. Yearning is like always having a little secret between you and a fantasy, and it can bind up all your energy. It can keep you in an unfulfilled state, or wishing for someone who is not appropriate or attainable. This can lead to obsession, or worse, yearning can be so comfortable (there is far less risk involved in love affairs of the mind), you miss the real love when it comes along.

Don't be too down on yourself; yearning is encouraged in our society. Women are brought up to feel incomplete without someone, so yearning seems normal. Try not to fall into this trap; it is a great power drain.

To keep from getting stuck, act on your yearning. Go back to the first three chapters of this book. You can also do a ritual for wholeness. (See Faye's WEB, page 37.) Breathe in all the aspects of your power and claim them. Invoke the goddess Isis, with her powers of the virgin, woman, crone.

WISE WORDS FOR THE MAIDEN

The maiden stood shyly outside the entrance of the pueblo. "Come in, child," the old woman called out to her. "I cannot see you against the bright sunlight."

The young woman hesitantly stepped through the bright turquoise doorway. "Grandmother, my mother says it is time I come and speak to you. But I do not know what to ask."

The old woman looked over the maid's ripening form and a smile creased her face. "Yes, it is time we talk for I cannot call you 'child' much longer. Come, hand me my yarn as I weave."

The maiden sat by the loom, her nerves calmed by the older woman's rhythmical movements. The woman gave her a sideways glance and began. "There are many young braves who stop to speak to you as you draw water from the river. Is there one who is special to you?"

The younger one blushed. "Well, I am very fond of your daughter's son."

The old woman nodded her concurrence. "A fine brave." Her voice took on a conspiratorial tone and she bent closer to the girl. "I have it from a good source that this brave is very fond of you, too." She smiled down at the maiden. "It is also a sign that it is time for you to realize your womanhood."

The maiden blushed. "Yes, I have felt the changes in me and seen how the men, even my own kin, no longer treat me like a child. But, I . . ."

The old woman leaned over and touched the young one's face. "Your beauty is surpassed only by your shyness. It is difficult to shed the protective cloak of childhood, especially for one who is used to hiding behind others. It is time for you to claim your own powers and become a woman."

The old woman leaned back in her chair with a faraway look in her eyes. "I remember my time. It was deep summer, I had done all the rituals to prepare myself and told my mother I was ready.

"On the night of the new moon, I went up the mountain to meditate and wait. A coyote howled in the distance and I saw a man walking out of the forest. I shook so hard my beaded fringe rattled. Without saying a word, he took my hands. His hands were warm and kind. I opened myself to him and I could feel him doing the same.

"He sat behind me, singing a low chant. Slowly, he began to unbraid my hair. His song and touch soothed me. When he finished, I took off my moccasins. Seems a silly thing to do, looking back on it, but he understood that I was accepting him as my lover.

"He gently removed my dress, taking time to stroke and caress me, all the while singing. That chant, it became like the beating of my heart. I trusted him completely. We made love twice. Once slow and rocking and the second wild and free, like elks in spring rut."

The old grandmother chuckled. "I think he was surprised the second time. Afterward, we lay in each other's arms until just before dawn, when the mists start to rise around the tall pines. He coiled my hair into the fashion of the women and put a spotted falcon's feather into it. He bowed before me and disappeared into the forest."

The young woman sat in awe. There was a long pause before she spoke. "Did you ever see him again?"

"Yes and no, for certainly he was a man from the village. You know the man paints his face and lets his hair flow loose. In the dark night with no moon, it was difficult to see his features. For days I looked at all the men, trying to guess, but soon I became more interested in the young men who came to court me.

"So my child, do you feel more ready now?"

The maiden smiled. "On my next flow, I will ask my mother to prepare the Becoming Ritual." She rose to leave and shyly nodded her thanks. "May I come and see you after that?"

The old woman smiled. "Oh, I have many stories and am always happy for a new ear. Come when you like. I am here."

EIGHT

Great Goddess: Faces of the Feminine

Remember when you were in second grade and someone told you that girls were made of sugar and spice and everything nice? Okay, now forget that and everything else you've been told about being born with a double-X chromosome.

We want you to know how the ancients saw the evolution of feminine power so you can have a more fulfilling experience, and if you really want sugar and spice, it's already included.

> There are three basic phases of the feminine:

Virgin: An open time, when your sexual desire awakens.
Woman: A more focused phase when sexual desire is fulfilled.
Sagesse: A reopening, and a culmination of sexual power.

Each phase leads to the next, as you have or will no doubt experience.

The Virgin Voyage

A girl embarks on her virgin voyage when she has her first crush. Unfamiliar sensual feelings start to emerge, she feels different in her own body. The openness of a child starts to shift into the more purposeful focus of an adult. Interests emerge, talent appears, and she wants to get kissed.

Virginity has little to do with the breaking of a membrane—it is about sexual flowering—taking place over a number of years. The Virgin Voyage begins the first time you think about boys to your first real relationship: the Awakening of The Woman. It is a passage, not an event.

A woman is no longer a virgin when she claims her sexuality, which can easily be done without having intercourse.

Having intercourse is your chance to experience masculine energy in a very different way. It is only part of a greater process, and it is not about losing anything. The only loss is girlhood.

Rituals for a maiden's first sexual experience were found in ancient India, Babylon, and of course, the spring fertility rites of Beltane celebrated in early western European civilization and now reminiscent in our May Day celebrations. In all cases, a young woman's first encounter would not be with her chosen lover but a "god" or a man in disguise. It was treated as a rite of passage, an induction, rather than a surrender or a deflowering.

Today, the ritual can be created to suit the individual. When she ("the virgin") is ready, whether or not there is someone in her life, she might do a simple prayer with a green candle to ask that this experience be one that brings her joy and knowledge and sharing. She can ask for an appropriate partner. Whether she has a date that leads to sex or not, this night marks the claiming of her full womanhood.

If the first sexual joining was not planned or isn't an experience that has meaning, it can be redone with someone else at another point. The hymen is not essential to the experience.

Technical Virgins

When you've been abstinent long enough to feel out of practice, you have entered the realm of the technical virgin. For some of us, it only takes a month, for others, a year, to reach this point. Expect to feel shy or uncertain, a bit like a teenager. Your skills are still there, you're just a little rusty.

If you don't miss sex, you're going through a dormant phase, which is perfectly natural. It would be fruitless and uncomfortable to work against it. However, if you're starting to feel sexual stirrings and there's no relief in sight, try releasing the dormancy.

EXERCISE TO RELEASE A DRY SPELL

Call on the Goddess Pele to help you. On a Friday during a waning moon, sprinkle just enough talcum powder on a surface to dust it. With your finger write the word *celibacy* in the powder, then blow the powder away. Light your white candle and say the following:

> Pele, join with me to welcome back my passion and fire.

Let the candle burn while you create the vision of the lover approaching you.

When your next consort shows up in reality, make use of your bewitching tools and techniques to ease you back into the sensual flow. And we caution you not to jump the first man who arrives; he's often a practice date, preceding a more appropriate match.

The Woman Stage

This a stage of your life focused on relationship, in work, family, and friends. It is natural to want a partner or mate. The phase of Woman is a phase of creation in all forms.

- Making a home
- Having children
- Exploring creative talents
- Self-expression
- Choosing to pursue a career

It is a rich and fecund period. It is the expression of self with and through others.

While our society might have lost respect for roots, home, and the earth, your inherent (and growing) connection to the Goddess gives you a natural desire for all of these things.

Most of this book addresses the stage of Woman. The only part we haven't discussed is childbearing, which is a natural expression of this phase. It's a choice that shouldn't be taken on by the Virgin and one that is surrendered by the Sagesse for greater freedom.

Sex for Conception

Sex does have a place beyond pleasure, when it serves the purpose of procreation. Of course, we have a strong opinion about this. We think couples should de-science sex for conception and look to nature and the magic arts to help guide their way. This is a particularly helpful method if you're having problems conceiving.

When you "wish" for a baby, the wish itself can become pressure; you could lose sight of that which makes a baby is your connection to each other. Using clinical tools can diminish both your powers and hence your connection—and often, magic works outside of science. You could get pregnant two weeks after you were "supposed to" have ovulated—it happens all the time.

Using procreating magic can be a more agreeable and certainly a more conscious experience.

Moon Cycles and Procreation

If you track your cycle (and if you don't, you should), you might already know your fertile times. We tend to get especially frisky around ovulation.

Beyond your cycle, however, there are six magical points in the year that encourage conception. These days are all new moons, which is when there is no moon in the sky (signified in your newspaper by a black moon). A new moon is a dark time, which creates enormous feminine power. It also initiates growth, being the point at which the moon turns to grow back to full. The most powerful new moons are in the signs of Taurus, Cancer, Leo, Scorpio, Capricorn, and Pisces. (See appendix A for finding specific dates.) You can plan some seductions around these dates.

BEFORE YOU DO IT

If you are trying to conceive, it is a good idea to take a sea salt bath to clear the energy of your womb. (You can both do this.)

Opening to Conception

Sit quietly before a bowl of water and some nuts in their casings. Place your hands on your root. Visualize a child, and breathe welcoming energy into your womb. Feel yourself as a vessel, able to hold and nourish a new being. Your consort can see himself as the giver of seed.

Lie side by side and visualize your energy centers connecting. See each color. Hold the heart connection and breathe into it. Visualize your love for each other as light going between your hearts.

When you make love, it is more about sharing and less about pleasure. Orgasm is not important. In fact it is much better to connect at the heart and use a rolling rhythm rather than a hard, forceful one. Continue to see yourself as a vessel.

After he releases, join for a few moments and hold each other, be tender and nurturing with each other.

Problems with Pregnancy?

There are some common nonphysical problems that can complicate pregnancy. Sometimes a man disconnects from you because you are having an experience he cannot share. You can feel less than attractive being large with child, and society can react negatively to the body of a pregnant woman. Pay attention to your feelings of self-esteem and shame.

> Call in the earth goddesses (Demeter, Gaia) to help.
>
> Pleasure each other in other ways.
>
> Stay conscious.
>
> Dress yourself with pride: flowing robes, flowers—a fantasy of ripeness, the epitome of womanhood.

Postchildbirth: The Baby Blues

You've just had a load of root energy leave your body. A lot of your nurturing/sensual energy is taken up by caring for your baby. And you're probably both exhausted.

POSTPARTUM COUPLING

Synchronize your breathing. Start by inhaling deep, vibrant red light into your own root center and exhaling into your partner's root center. When that feels complete, move up to your heart center and do the same, using green light.

It is best to ease back into lovemaking. To think it will be an easy reconnection might be expecting too much. It might be painful for you at first but joyful for him and his reconnection with you.

Watch for self-doubt, beratement, and guilt, which can happen as a result of feeling as if there's something wrong with you for not being aroused. This prolongs the process of reconnection. The best thing to do is have someone else take care of the child for an evening so that you can just be alone with each other. Take time to be sensual with your lover—taking time doesn't have to mean sex. It will help rekindle and reconnect your passions.

Beyond Childbearing

Whether or not you choose to have children, make sure that you explore the many facets of the Woman phase. Explore relationships and play with your creativity, don't just work and watch TV! It will not serve you or your loved ones to deny your potential, and it can make menopause uncomfortable as you won't be ready for it.

During this phase a woman usually wants to explore her options regarding relationships, her home, family, and creativity.

To complete the phase of Woman without having a sense of missed opportunities, integrate activities into your life that you find fulfilling. Consider taking a class, making new friends, volunteering, etc.

The Sagesse

Crone was a word in ancient cultures that used to imply a powerful, respected woman. She is portrayed as the wise woman and healer. To avoid the negative connotations, we've renamed the Crone, "Sagesse" from the Latin root *"sapere,"* which means to be wise.

Modern society treats older women like children: dependent, useless, nonsexual, which forces the Sagesse to be a Virgin again. Actually, the Sagesse contains the experience of both Virgin and Woman and carries it further into the mystical, spiritual side. The Sagesse has more freedom than the Woman and more wisdom than the girl.

Sagesse is about personal power ripening. A mature woman's focus seems to trade places with that of the man. You'll see men of the same age focusing more on relationships while the Sagesse is less consumed by them. There can be a balancing of interests between the sexes.

In earlier societies, the Sagesse would guide and teach young girls in both earth-connected and spirit-connected skills. They are open like the Virgin, and less narrowly focused than the mother. The Sagesse is freed from the insecurities and inexperience of youth and the nurturing, relationship drive of the Woman. She has the time and the ability to explore the inner and outer worlds.

The more connected you are with your sensuality, feminine power, and its expression, the less difficult claiming the Sagesse (menopause) will be. If you have denied your femininity in some way, you might have problems with this transition.

The Sexy Sagesse

Just because you don't ovulate doesn't mean you're not hot. Your lust might not be as urgent as it was in youth, but it is far from gone.

Mating is now solely for pleasure, not for procreation. Think of it: no more birth control, no more anxiety. There is more time for you.

Sound great? Yep. Now you just have to get there. Time for a pause—menopause.

Menopause Madness

The rule of menopause is to expect the unexpected. It may feel as if you're going through all the cycles of the feminine simultaneously.

Menopause is resisted in our society partly because of the stigma to being "old" and past childbearing years. As a reaction, women try to delay it, uncomfortably holding back their force.

Any savvy sorceress understands that this is a passage that honors the reproductive system and celebrates the freedom of being "period free"—a time of shifting into deeper feminine power.

Since it is sometimes a wobbly time sexually, it helps a great deal to meditate on your root center. Clear the bottom two centers—to end the mother phase. At the same time, scent and open your third center, where the energy is shifting—this is your power center. Your energy is now moving up here from the root. You may gain weight if you don't open to your power.

It is better to stay in sync with the season during this transition. Try to take vacations in places where the seasons are similar to where you live. For instance, if you live in the north, it is not a good time to winter in Florida. Your whole body rhythm is shifting and you are too sensitive to adjust easily to such dramatic change.

Expect times when you won't be interested in sex. It's a more internal time when you might not want to be as active or social as before. We're told some women cry more easily or become emotionally unstable. It's only temporary. Estrogen replacement seems to be very helpful.

It is a good time to ask your consort to hold you. You are giving over being the nurturer (whether or not you've had children).

POSTMENOPAUSE PEP-UPS

> After menopause, meditate on the root, masturbate, and if you are not with a consort, have massages, saunas, etc., to keep your sensual and physical pleasures alive. Try to sense the shift in your root energy. It is no longer for reproduction; it is simply for pleasure's sake, and it may take different forms.
>
> This change happens to men, too, though without the formality of menopause.

Sex is often better after menopause. Most of the shame in sex is gone and you know what you want. You also have freedom (and relief) from birth control.

Your rhythms are much more subtle and you may have to pay more attention to your needs. You can honor your body changes the way you can honor it for pregnancy. Your inner light takes over more and more—hopefully you have nurtured it all along. You won't have to behave as you did at twenty-two (you won't want to) because you won't have the hormonal push to do so. (Hanging out in a bar with a martini and a cigarette won't be as appealing.)

RESURRECTING THE GODDESS

Tap into your power, whatever phase you're in. The Goddess will answer you. She is your source. This is a good all-purpose booster. In any situation, you can invoke a goddess to bring back some power you may feel you've lost. Appeal to one or more goddesses; have their names handy. (Consult goddess chart in Chapter 4 and Appendix B.)

1. On a waxing moon, in your favorite room, have flowers and a bowl of water, a flame, and some scent (any fragrance you like).

2. Place a power object (something you're proud of) before you.

3. Sit in front of the flame.

4. Draw the energy up from the earth into your root, weave it through each center, and then release it from the crown.

5. Chant or say aloud, like a mantra, the name(s) of the goddess(es) you have chosen and your own name.*

*The Goddess you choose is a highly personal choice. Study the Goddesses in Appendix B to understand which will help you realize your goals. This is an important part of the mystical process.

6. Aloud, say you recognize your own powers and call on those goddesses to help you with their strength and wisdom.

7. Fill your heart with that intention, then place your hands on the ground to anchor those qualities within yourself. Say: So be it. And so it is.

APPENDIX A

The Moon's Magic

Moon Cycles: A Review

The moon is associated with the feminine (and its counterpart, the sun, with the masculine). The cycle of the moon has long been used as a metaphor for the feminine cycle.

When the moon is approaching full, it is called a *waxing moon.* The waxing moon is related to ovulation and fertility. The peak of the waxing phase is the *full moon*; its light fades until the *new moon* (no moon in the sky). The process of the fading moon is called the *waning moon.* The new moon is associated with menstruation, or the release of the energy from the full moon.

After the new moon, the light returns in the waxing

phase again. And so goes the moon cycle and the cycles of women.

The Moon's Day-to-Day Influences

The moon travels through the entire zodiac in every monthly cycle. (The sun does the same over the course of the year.) As it passes through each sign, it brings out different impulses, atmospheres, and energy that can affect both our sexual drives and our general moods.

To know what astrological sign the moon is in, you'll need a lunar calendar (we use the Celestial Pocket Calendar) or a witch's almanac. Although it takes some time to get used to reading these calendars, they become indispensable once you discover how beneficial it can be to plan according to the moon's phases.

The following chart is a general overview of the moon's influence over us as it travels through each sign.

Moon in . . .	**Influence**
Aries	Aggressive, energetic behavior
Taurus	Earthy, nonverbal, desire to shop
Gemini	Chatty, social, flirtatious
Cancer	Sentimental, nurturing
Leo	Partying, voguing, glowing
Virgo	Urge to clean, figure things out
Libra	Desire to be with loved one, to talk

Moon in . . .	Influence
Scorpio	Need for privacy, intimacy
Sagittarius	Urge to try something new, explore
Capricorn	Acquisitiveness, grounded
Aquarius	Spacey, dreamy, creative urges
Pisces	Romantic, vulnerable feelings

Ritual Moons

There are times when a full or new moon is more appropriate to a given spell or enchantment; for instance, a new moon is much better to induce fertility and a full moon is great for fantasy night.

Basically, the new moon will be in the same sign as the sun. The full moon will be in the sign that is "opposite" it or six months away. Use the following chart as a quick reference.

For instance, you are considering a full moon "fantasy" night in July. If you want to use the full moon to its greatest power, just look up its sign and note its element. The full moon in July is in Capricorn, which is an earth sign. Thus, it's a good time to try physical sensuality. A full moon in a water sign is best used for role playing and other illusions.

There is no need to memorize this. Check your local paper for the new or full moons and find the sign in the chart below.

The Sun is in	Sign of full moon	Sign of new moon
Aries (3/20–4/19)	Libra	Aries
Taurus (4/20–5/19)	Scorpio	Taurus
Gemini (5/20–6/20)	Sagittarius	Gemini
Cancer (6/21–7/21)	Capricorn	Cancer
Leo (7/22–8/21)	Aquarius	Leo
Virgo (8/22–9/21)	Pisces	Virgo
Libra (9/22–10/21)	Aries	Libra
Scorpio (10/22–11/21)	Taurus	Scorpio
Sagittarius (11/22–12/20)	Gemini	Sagittarius
Capricorn (12/21–1/19)	Cancer	Capricorn
Aquarius (1/20–2/19)	Leo	Aquarius
Pisces (2/20–3/19)	Virgo	Pisces

APPENDIX B

Sexual Aspects of Goddesses Around the World

Aeval (Ireland) Fairy Queen of Munster, goddess of love and sexuality, magic, and things of small size. Aeval, on hearing complaints from her women about the sexual performances of their mates, ruled that men must learn to be more creative and open in their sexual practices.

Anahita (Persia) Her name means without blemish; she is goddess of the moon, love, sexuality, water, selflessness, and war. A mother goddess, she fertilizes the force of the earth and cleanses the womb. She is associated with orgiastic religion and sacred sexuality. In Zoroastrian teachings, she is a goddess of war and is seen driving a chariot pulled by four white horses—symbolizing wind, rain, clouds, and hail.

Aphrodite (Greece) Aphrodite rose to the surface of the ocean, the essence of feminine beauty, perfect in her pure features, beautiful body, gleaming fair hair, and grace. Aphrodite always exudes an aura of seduction about her, with a sweet smile on her face. She is the mistress of seductive conversation, gracious laughter, sweet deceits, and the charms and delights of love.

Artemis (Greece) Goddess of the chase and of the moon (Apollo, her twin brother, was a sun god), she appears as a young woman accompanied by a dog, sometimes a deer, holding a bow and arrow. She was the goddess and mother of wild animals and personifies that untamed animal side of human nature. She was also the virgin goddess of childbirth, whose own ability to express abandonment at the forces of nature helped women surrender in childbirth.

Astarte (Phoenicia) Astarte, meaning "Queen of Heaven," is goddess of fertility, love, and sacred sexuality. She is associated with heaven and hell, moon and night, mother and guardian. Also a goddess of water, she was a guardian of ships and sailors. She corresponds to Ishtar of Babylon and Aphrodite of Greece.

Athene (Greece) Despite her being a warrior goddess, she is also goddess of the arts of peace and of prudent intelligence. She was the patron of architects and sculptors and spinners and weavers, and excels as the working woman. She protects horses and oxen, and her wisdom earned her the name of counselor goddess and Goddess of the Assembly. Her emblem is the owl. She is represented sheathed in tight drapery, holding a shield and spear.

Bastet (Egypt) Cat goddess of pleasure who loved music and dance, she protected men against contagious diseases and evil spirits. Originally she was a lioness goddess, personifying the fertilizing warmth of the sun. Later her sacred animal became the cat, and she is represented as a cat-headed woman.

Benten (Japan) Buddhist goddess of happiness, luck, wealth, the arts, water, reptiles, and the sea. Sometimes seen as a dragon woman.

Bridgit (Irish) Bridgit, meaning "High One," is a mother goddess of healing, poetry, fertility, and fire, whose attributes include household affairs and ceremonies. She survived Christianity as Saint Bridgit (or Bride). She was worshipped solely by women.

Cybele (Asia Minor) Cybele is an ancient Great Mother goddess of fertility and wildlife (connecting her to Artemis). She is guardian of the dead, Goddess of the Mountain or "the Lady of Ida," derived from a great mountain in western Anatolia. She is a lion goddess often enthroned with lions or leopards by her side.

Demeter (Greece) Representing the fertile and cultivated soil, she is a virgin goddess of the fruits and riches of the fields. She presides over the harvest and is usually crowned with shafts of wheat, and a veil hanging down her back, wearing a long robe and holding a scepter. Her severe beauty is softened by her golden hair, likened to ripened grain.

Estsanatlehi (Navaho) Estsanatlehi means "self-renewing one." Goddess of transformation, immortality, time, and magic, she can transform herself through the three stages of the feminine—Virgin, Woman, and Sagesse. She controls fertility and sterility. She is the essence of death and rebirth.

Gaia (Greece) Gaia is the great goddess who gave birth to existence, who makes children and bounty manifest, creator of the universe and the first race of gods and humans. Famed also as an oracle (hers was at Delphi before it passed to Apollo), she is the "universal mother." Gaia was commonly represented as a gigantic woman.

Guanyin (China) Goddess of mercy, compassion, protector of children and women, she bestows good health and fertility. She is associated with knowledge, physical strength, and goodness. Guanyin is also associated with sound and called "the melodious voice."

Hathor (Egypt) Goddess of the sky, dance, music, and love, she is represented as a cow (the ancient Egyptians believed in the concept of the sky as a cow). She was usually shown in human form, though, wearing a disc between two cow horns on her head, a sign of her having raised the youthful sun into the sky by means of her horns.

Hecate (Greece) A moon goddess, and a deity of the Underworld, she was known as Queen of the Night and often took the form of a crone goddess. She bestows riches, victory, and wisdom to mankind, presides over knowledge and education, protects her followers from evil, and is called the Invincible Queen. She is also a goddess of enchantments and magic charms and appears at night accompanied by her retinue of dogs.

Hera (Greece) Originally queen of the sky and married to Zeus, she presides over all phases of feminine existence, although she is mainly goddess of marriage and maternity. She represents the idealized wife and the Woman deified. Normally she was depicted as a young, fully developed woman of chaste and severe beauty, crowned with a diadem. She is often characterized by a cuckoo and a pomegranate, symbolizing conjugal love and fruitfulness.

Hestia (Greece) Hestia means "hearth," and she was goddess of the home, and protector of the house, the family, and the city. She was a fire goddess and was associated with the fire at the center of the earth and the earth itself.

Innana/Ishtar (Babylonia/Sumeria—Mesopotamia) Innana, known also as Ishtar, is goddess of fertility, love, war, and the divine personification of the planet Venus. She arouses amorous desire in all creatures. As a lunar goddess, she breathes life into us as the moon waxes and withdraws as the moon wanes. Innana is the law giver and also a war goddess known for her courage. She is often represented standing on a chariot drawn by seven lions, with a bow in her hands.

Isis (Egypt) Queen of the stars, goddess of life and healing, protector of the dead, mother goddess. Isis was the symbolic mother, representing the fertile plains of Egypt. She was the lamenting goddess, known for her great knowledge of magic, and the patron divinity of travelers. She helped civilize Egypt by teaching women to spin flax, weave cloth, and grind wheat. She also taught men the art of curing disease and, by instituting the marriage, domesticity. She took on the symbols of Hathor, with the horns and disc on her head, or was represented with a throne on her head, or a cow's head set on a human body.

Lakshmi (India) Brilliant and perfumed goddess of fortune and prosperity, luck, wealth, healing, beauty, and a primordial creator of life. She was born from the churning of the ocean at the beginning of time, often portrayed holding a lotus.

Macha (Irish) Celtic goddess of fertility. In mythology she appears also as a warrior queen who did not fight with mortal weapons, but used supernatural powers and shape-shifting, taking on the shape of other animals.

Pele (Hawaii) Goddess of love, sexuality, the earth, volcanic fire, nature, disorder, beauty, and ugliness. Pele can appear as an ugly or beautiful woman.

Rhiannon (British) Welsh fertility goddess of charisma and domesticated animals, she is an enchantress who rides a white mare, followed by birds that proclaim the seasons.

Sarasvati (India) Sarasvati means "the Flowing One." A river goddess of music, wisdom, and knowledge, associated with fertility and wealth. Sarasvati is depicted as a beautiful, graceful, pale-skinned woman sitting on a peacock, with a crescent moon adorning her brow.

Sekhmet (Egypt) Sekhmet means "Mighty One." She was goddess of war and spread fear everywhere. She was represented as a lioness or a woman with a lion's head. She was also regarded as the one "great of magic," whose knowledge of sorcery gave her a place in the service of healing.

Ushas (India) Goddess of the dawn, dressed in rose-colored robes and golden veils, she is born anew each morning, young and yet old, since she is immortal. She is a fresh and beautiful young girl, a bejeweled dancing girl, a wife dressed in magnificent clothes awaiting her husband. Always smiling, irresistible in her charms, she half opens her veils to reveal treasures in her folds. She travels in a shining chariot drawn by cows or horses. She gives light to the world and is the life and health of all things.

Wadjet (Egypt) Snake goddess, Wadjet means "the green one," or in ancient Egypt another term for the cobra. She was Queen of the Gods of Egypt associated with justice, heaven and hell, time, and ceremonies. She was the serpent equated with the royal uraeus (snake on the Egyptian head-dress), and appeared as a winged and crowned cobra. Wadjet was a symbol of growth and the national Goddess of Lower Egypt.

Xochiquetzal (Aztec) Meaning "flower feather," she is a goddess of pleasure, beauty, love, sexuality, flowers, the earth, and a mother-guardian figure. Much loved by women, she is connected to childbirth and weaving.

APPENDIX C

Meditation

Guidelines for Beginners

- **Three times a week is a good frequency for starters.**
- **Twenty minutes is a good average session, but don't be surprised if you need to build up to this level.** Begin with what you can do—five or ten minutes is better than nothing.
- **There is no "right" or "wrong" way to meditate.** However, if you find a particular method unsettling, stop. (Unsettling is not the same as anxious. Anxiety is normal when you try to calm your mind.)
- **Everybody's mind wanders, even the most consistent, experienced meditators.** Just keep bringing yourself back to the meditation.

- **No one meditates perfectly all the time.** Bliss can be experienced at any part of your practice, even your first time. Just know that your meditation experience will constantly evolve and go through cycles.
- **Set the mood and scene for meditating.**
    1. Take a bath before meditating.
    2. Light a candle and/or incense.
    3. Play soothing music in the background. Many music stores carry tapes and CDs made especially for meditation.
    4. Hold a crystal or gem.
    5. Create a special corner with power objects, flowers, a representation of the Goddess and elements.
- **Meditate sitting up not lying down.** You don't want to fall asleep. (However, you may find meditating lying down helpful for getting to sleep at night.)

Overview

There are many ways to meditate, and this overview provides you with a summary of some of the more popular methods. Try those that appeal to you and stick with the one that works best.

Breath Awareness

All you need to do for this meditation is breathe. Close your eyes and concentrate on the sensation of your breath as it enters and leaves your nostrils.

You are not trying to control your breathing, just be conscious of it. When thoughts wander through your mind and demand attention, let them go and bring your attention back to your breathing. The same with background noise, discomfort, etc. Try to let them fade away.

Focus on the feeling of your breath in your nose and lips. Is it light, heavy, ticklish, rushing? The possibilities are endless. This will help occupy your ever-restless mind.

If you have trouble concentrating just on the breath, try counting them from one to ten—over and over. Or deliberately take in a deep breath and bring yourself back.

As you become more practiced, you can visualize taking clear, healing energy into your body on the inhalation and releasing toxins and stress on the exhalation. You can also use this as a warm-up to clear your mind when you are looking for intuitive answers to questions.

Mantra

A mantra is a word or a phrase that is repeated over and over. It gives your "monkey mind," as some traditions call it, something to do while you tune in to your Inner Self.

The words used are also believed to have a connection to a deeper source that gives them a special power. The best-known version of this practice is Transcendental Meditation. Classes are available in TM, Zen, and yoga, and they can be helpful for beginners.

The mantra is a good tool for experimenting with extended meditation. It also becomes a touchstone over time that you can use through the day to bring you back to a clear, meditative focus.

Some forms use a string of beads that you hold in your hand. As you recite the mantra, you move to the next bead, like rosary beads. It links the body and the mind, which sometimes makes it easier to shift into meditation.

The mantra, like breathing, changes with your state of mind, sometimes loud, sometimes delicate, sometimes elusive. With practice, it will run by itself, needing only occasional prompting.

Ram or *Om* are good words to try. Or you can use a word or phrase that speaks to your higher sense of self, such as "love," "forgiveness," or "May I be at peace."

Contemplation

Reading uplifting or spiritual books, praying, and being in nature are all types of contemplation. Many of us do this without labeling it meditation, but that's what it is—a calm, clear space that gives you a little more peace.

To try this, pick a writer you find inspirational and whose work you like reading. (This is not supposed to be torturous or boring.) Thoreau, Merton, Watts, Fox are well known, but there are thousands from whom to choose. As you read, let their words sink in. When something strikes you as particularly powerful, take a moment and think about it. Reflect. What is it teaching you? How does it relate to your life? Return to the thought during the day.

If you are lucky enough to live in a natural setting, mother nature can provide you with plenty of opportunities for meditating. Walk, breathing the air and feeling the earth under your feet. Connect with it and all the plants and living beings around you. When you are inspired to stop and sit, do so. Trees are great teachers. Sit under one and sees what it says.

Heart Meditation

This technique, as stated in the name, comes from, and speaks to, the heart. It is less impersonal than many other forms. It uses contemplation or prayer while sitting with the picture of someone or a symbol you are drawn to. The heart meditation opens the way to greater intimacy.

To do this meditation, place the picture or object in front of you. Imagine it entering into you and being held in your heart. Let yourself feel it radiate compassion to you. After you start to feel connected, you can ask questions, speak with it or simply sit with it.

You can also sing the personal object's name. It may feel silly at first but the sound is very powerful. You'll be amazed how much better you'll feel. Don't be afraid to be loud or unmusical. It is perfectly okay to howl if you want to. It should express how you feel in that moment from your heart and from your guts. Like the beads and mantra combo, it gives it another level of experience.

Over time you may use different symbols for your key to the heart. Eventually you'll probably find yourself doing it without an outside prompt.

VISUALIZATION

Sometimes called creative visualization, this technique is similar to fantasies and daydreams so all of us are already halfway there. All you have to add is focus and purpose. (Fantasizing about Brad Pitt, however juicy it might be, does not qualify as a focus.) You can use it to seek answers, explore a situation, get inspiration.

To start, you might buy a tape in a New Age bookstore, or make one yourself. Begin with some relaxation and then "go" to a place that you imagine, somewhere you feel open and safe. It can be imagined or a spot you have visited. You can call on your guides or sit there silently, in your mind's eye, and see what answers surface.

Try building the meditation around a current issue such as love, health, prosperity. Doing this over time can give you a lot of information and help. With practice, you will not need a tape.

This technique is probably best done after you have learned some other form of meditation so you already know how to go within.

Movement

For some people, sitting still is torture. If you need to move, follow your natural inclination and use that as your starting point. This is true of any technique. You will be a thousand times more likely to do and stick with something you enjoy.

There are many formalized movement meditations—T'ai Chi, martial arts, yoga. If you don't believe changing the position of your body is powerful, try making tightly clenched fists with your hands. Now put your hands lightly together in prayer position or extend them before you slightly cupped. You'll notice immediately the surge of energy in your hands and body.

Movement meditations can be done at any time—running, walking, dancing. It is the purposeful attention to the movement that differentiates it from everyday activities.

Try a Zen walking meditation. Hands loosely clasped in front of you, walk very deliberately. Feel every shift of your body. This will naturally slow you down, so don't try it when you are running to catch the bus!

Mindfulness

Mindfulness is paying complete attention to one thing. Sound is particularly easy to work with. Simply sit and listen.

You will begin to hear various sounds rising and falling around you.

It can also be done with an object, say a flower or a crystal. Simply sit and look at it, eyes softly focused. Observe the object, do not label it. It is not purple or round or glistening. It just is.

You can listen to yourself, homing in on the constantly shifting thoughts, emotions, sensations, images that all come together to make up your essence.

When you focus this way, you will find yourself in the flow of life—which is really constant transformation and change. Being mindful can be particularly useful when you are feeling stuck or overwhelmed.

Suggested Reading

For Further Reading about the Goddess

Goddesses in World Mythology, a Biographical Dictionary by Martha Ann and Dorothy Myers Imel.

An Illustrated Dictionary of the Gods and Symbols of Ancient Egypt by Manfred Lurker.

Larrouse Encyclopedia of Mythology.

The Myth of the Goddess, Evolution of an Image by Anne Baring, and Jules Cashford.

The Once and Future Goddess by Elinor W. Gaddon.

Goddess for Every Season by Nancy Blair.

Ancient Mirrors of Womanhood by Merlin Stone.

For Sexy Inspiration

203 Ways to Please a Man in Bed by Olivia St. Claire.

The Art of Sexual Ecstasy by Margo Anand.

The Art of Sexual Magic by Margo Anand.

Sex Tips for Girls by Cynthia Heimel.

The Erotic Edge by Connie Barbah.

Good Girl's Guide to Great Sex by Debbie Peterson and Tom King.

For More Spellbinding Information

Simple Spells for Love: Ancient Practices for Emotional Fulfillment by Barrie Dolnick.

Magical Herbalism by Scott Cunningham.

Linda Goodman's Love Signs by Linda Goodman.

Pocket Astrologer by Jim Maynard.

For More on Feminine Power

The Spiral Dance by Starhawk.

Women Who Run with the Wolves by Clarissa Pinkola Estes.

The Chalice and the Blade by Riane Eisler.

The Holy Book of Women's Mysteries by Zsuzanna Budapest.

Crossing to Avalon by Jean Shinoda Bolen.

The Way of the Woman by Helen M. Luke.

The Goddess Within by Ellen Barker Woolgin and Roger Woolgin.

The Crone by Barbara Walker.

Women's Rituals by Barbara Walker.

More on the Chakras

Anatomy of Spirit by Caroline Myess.

Wheels of Light by Roseanne Bruyere.

Wheels of Life by Judith Llewellyn.

More on Meditation

Journey of Awakening by Ram Dass.

How to Mediate by Lawrence LeShan.